The Eschatological Community
of the Dead Sea Scrolls

SOCIETY OF BIBLICAL LITERATURE
MONOGRAPH SERIES

Adela Yarbro Collins, Editor
Edward F. Campbell, Jr., Associate Editor

Number 38
THE ESCHATOLOGICAL COMMUNITY
OF THE DEAD SEA SCROLLS
A Study of the
Rule of the Congregation

by
Lawrence H. Schiffman

Lawrence H. Schiffman

THE ESCHATOLOGICAL COMMUNITY
OF THE DEAD SEA SCROLLS
A Study of the Rule of the Congregation

Scholars Press
Atlanta, Georgia

The Eschatological Community of the Dead Sea Scrolls
A Study of the Rule of the Congregation

by
Lawrence H. Schiffman

© 1989
Society of Biblical Literature

Library of Congress Cataloging-in-Publication Data

Schiffman, Lawrence H.
   The eschatological community of the Dead Sea scrolls : a study of
the rule of the congregation / Lawrence H. Schiffman.
       p.   cm.—(The Society of Biblical Literature monograph
series : no. 38)
   Bibliography: p.
   Includes indexes.
   ISBN 1-55540-329-8 (alk. paper).—ISBN 1-55540-330-1 (pbk. :
alk. paper)
   1. Manual of discipline.   2. Qumran community.   I. Title.
II. Series.
BM488.M3S35   1989   89-6091
296.1′55—dc 19   CIP

Printed in the United States of America

CONTENTS

ABBREVIATIONS

1QH	*Hodayot (Thanksgiving Scroll)*
11QTemple	*Temple Scroll*
1QM	*Scroll of the War of the Sons of Light against the Sons of Darkness*
1QS	*Manual of Discipline (Rule of the Community)*
1QSa	*Rule of the Congregation*
1QSb	*Rule of Benedictions*
AJSR	*Association for Jewish Studies Review*
Ant.	Josephus, *Antiquities*
BASOR	*Bulletin of the American Schools of Oriental Research*
BDB	F. Brown, S. Driver, and C. Briggs, *A Hebrew and English Lexicon of the Old Testament*
b.	*Babylonian Talmud*
CBQ	*Catholic Biblical Quarterly*
DJD	Discoveries in the Judaean Desert
EJ	*Encyclopedia Judaica*
GKC	*Gesenius' Hebrew Grammar*, ed. E. Kautzsch, tr. A. E. Cowley
HTR	*Harvard Theological Review*
JBL	*Journal of Biblical Literature*
JSS	*Journal of Jewish Studies*
J.W.	Josephus, *Jewish War*
LCL	Loeb Classical Library
m.	*Mishnah*
NTS	*New Testament Studies*
RB	*Revue biblique*
RQ	*Revue de Qumran*
t.	*Tosefta*
VT	*Vetus Testamentum*
y.	*Palestinian Talmud*

PREFACE

This monograph is a continuation of my work on Jewish law as reflected in the Qumran corpus. My previous studies dealt with the manner in which the Qumran sect derived its law, and the basis on which the authority of the law was established. I also investigated the ways in which the legal system of the Dead Sea sect was intimately connected with the organization of the group in the present age. This study moves further into the areas of law in which the sect's eschatological aspirations merged with their legal teachings. Indeed, we will see that the messianic age is to be one of perfect legal observance and ritual purity. In this way, it is law which defines messianism. At the same time, the sect's dreams of a future age shaped the law in the present, pre-messianic era.

Some of my research on the *Rule of the Congregation* (1QSa) appeared in preliminary form in the *Proceedings of the American Academy for Jewish Research* and in *Biblical Archaeology Today*, ed. J. Amitai (Jerusalem: Israel Exploration Society, 1985). In the present work I provide a study of the entire document, analyzed within the context of the history of the various manifestations of Jewish messianism and Jewish law. It is my hope that this study will succeed in demonstrating the nexus of law and eschatology in the teachings of the Qumran sect.

Many have contributed to the completion of this monograph. Professor Baruch A. Levine of New York University has as always been a constant source of advice and encouragement. Professor Francis E. Peters, also of New York University, has greatly deepened my perspective on the cultural context in which the texts discussed here were written. I continue to learn much from my colleagues in the Skirball Department of Hebrew and Judaic Studies, the Department of Near Eastern Languages and Literatures, and the Hagop Kevorkian Center for Near Eastern Studies at New York University. It is these colleagues and our students who provide the atmosphere in which research can flourish. Dr. Philip Miller, Librarian of the Klau Library of the Hebrew Union College–Jewish Institute of Religion in New York, was most gracious in his assistance.

My wife Marlene R. Schiffman, Judaica and Reference Librarian at the Klau Library of Hebrew Union College–Jewish Institute of Religion in New York, helped greatly with the preparation of the manuscript, made many important suggestions, and compiled the indexes. Her help and support for my research has been indispensable. This volume is dedicated to the memory of her parents who were imbued with respect for Judaic scholarship and who took great pride in my publications. יהי זכרם ברוך, may their memory be for a blessing!

INTRODUCTION

The Concept of Messianism

Central to the development of post-biblical Judaism in all its various manifestations has been the messianic idea. Roughly stated, this concept refers to the eventual coming of a redeemer, a descendant of David, who is expected to bring about major changes in the nature of life in this world, changes which include the attainment of such goals as world peace, prosperity, and the elimination of evil and misfortune. Essential to the messianic idea in Judaism is the expectation of the reestablishment of the ancient glories of the Davidic kingdom in the Land of Israel. It must be firmly emphasized that Jewish messianism is this-worldly and expresses itself in concrete terms. The rise in the spiritual level of humanity which will attend the messianic era is to be both cause and effect of the ingathering of Israel and the recognition of Israel's God by all the peoples of the earth.

The foregoing is, of course, a sweeping generalization. The messianic idea in Judaism has a complex history. The matter is further complicated by the simultaneous existence, even within the same strain of Judaism, of various views of messianism. Certain patterns or trends of messianic thought can be distinguished, and a historical discussion of them will lead to a more detailed and more accurate picture.

We shall be guided here by the programmatic essay of G. Scholem.[1] Scholem set out to understand the dominant trends in Jewish messianism and the tension between them. He noted the poles of restorative vs. utopian messianism. The restorative seeks to bring back the ancient glories, whereas the utopian constructs a view of an even better future, one that surpasses all that ever came before. The restorative can be described as a much more

---

[1] G. Scholem, "Toward an Understanding of the Messianic Idea in Judaism," *The Messianic Idea in Judaism* (New York: Schocken Books, 1971) 1–36. See also S. Talmon, "Types of Messianic Expectation at the Turn of the Era," *King, Cult and Calendar in Ancient Israel* (Jerusalem: Magnes, 1987) 203–5. Contrast the approach of W. S. Green, "Introduction: Messianism in Judaism: Rethinking the Question," *Judaisms and Their Messiahs at the Turn of the Christian Era* (ed. J. Neusner, W. S. Green and E. Frerichs; Cambridge: Cambridge University Press, 1987) 1–13. An article by the writer continues the analysis presented here through the rabbinic period (L. H. Schiffman, "The Concept of the Messiah in Second Temple and Rabbinic Literature," *Review and Expositor* 84 [1987] 235–46).

1

rational messianism, expecting only the improvement and perfection of the present world. The utopian is much more apocalyptic in character, looking forward to vast catastrophic changes in the world with the coming of the messianic age.[2] It is not that either of these approaches can exist independently of the other; rather, both are found in the messianic aspirations of the various Jewish groups. But the balance or creative tension between these tendencies is what determines the character of the messianism in question.

The Biblical Background

Although we are concerned mainly with the messianism of the Second Temple period, the background of this concept in the Hebrew Bible must be sketched briefly. Indeed, all the concepts of messianism in Judaism may be seen as interpretations of the traditions of the Hebrew Scriptures.

The messianic ideal is based on the doctrine of the Bible that David and his descendants were chosen by God to rule over Israel until the end of time (2 Sam 7; 23:1–3, 5). God also gave the Davidic house dominion over alien peoples (2 Sam 22:44–51 = Ps 18:44–51; Ps 2). 2 Sam 22:50–51 (= Ps 18:50–51) speaks of King David as the "anointed one" (משיח) whose descendants shall rule forever. Kings were anointed as part of a rite of appointment or consecration.

With the split of the kingdom after the death of Solomon and the attendant diminution of the scope of the Davidic empire, there arose a hope for the restoration of the ancient glories of the past. This reunited Davidic monarchy would also control the neighboring territories originally part of the Davidic and Solomonic empires. Isaiah emphasizes the qualities of the future Davidic monarch, the most prominent of which is the justness of his rule (Isa 11:1–9).[3]

Somewhat related to the question of messianism, certainly with the benefit of hindsight, is the biblical notion of the Day of the Lord. This is the concept found in prophetic literature that at some certain, though as yet unrevealed time, God is expected to punish the wicked and bring about the triumph of justice and righteousness.[4] The most prominent feature of this notion is the underlying sense of doom, including the motifs of wailing and darkness. The prophets assert that this day is near. This concept was already well established by the time of Amos, in the earliest years of the literary prophets. Apparently (cf. Amos 5:18–20), the popular view was an optimistic

---

[2] On the apocalyptic genre, see J. J. Collins, *The Apocalyptic Imagination* (New York: Crossroad, 1984) 1–32.

[3] H. L. Ginsberg, "Messiah," *EJ* 11. 1407–8; cf. S. Mowinckel, *He that Cometh* (trans. G. W. Anderson; Oxford: Basil Blackwell, 1956) 2–186.

[4] Cf. Isa 13:6–13; Joel 1:15; 2:1; 3:4; 4:14; Amos 5:18–20; Obad 15; Zeph 1:17–18; Mal 3:23. See also Isa 2:12; Ezek 30:3; Zech 14:1–9.

one which presumably had patriotic overtones. It may be that this concept is to be connected with the notion of a divine warrior who reveals his will through victory in battle (cf. Ezek 13:5). The wicked will be punished, justice will be established and the destiny of the world will be changed. God is certain to act to destroy evil and exalt righteousness, in a sudden and decisive manner. This was, for the prophets, a source of intense dread as widespread destruction was expected.[5]

Let us pause to consider the biblical material from the First Temple period in light of the messianic typologies proposed by Scholem. The notion of a return to the bygone days of Davidic rule and to the place of Israel as world-power typifies the restorative tendency. That which was but is no more is to be again. The notion of the Day of the Lord, the catastrophic upheaval which is to usher in a new age, is utopian. It calls for the utter destruction of all evil and wickedness, something never before seen in the history of humanity. That which never was is to be. These two approaches together will mold the eschatological speculation of all Jewish groups. Yet it is important to notice that in the Hebrew Scriptures these ideas are still separate. It is their combination in Second Temple times which will unleash the powerful forces eventually to propel the Jews through a series of revolts against Rome and to lead the Christians to the acceptance of a messianic figure.

The Second Temple Period

The very same two trends are visible in the Second Temple period. Restorative and utopian views of the Jewish future vied with one another as part of the melting pot of ideologies which make up the varieties of Judaism in this era.[6] The restorative trend emphasized primarily the reconstitution of the Davidic dynasty, whereas the destruction of the wicked is the main object of the more utopian and apocalyptic varieties that take their cue from the notion of the Day of the Lord.

In early Second Temple times, the prophets Haggai and Zechariah expected that the Davidic kingdom would be renewed under Zerubbabel. At the same time, Zechariah expected two "messianic" figures, the high priest and the messianic king (Zech 6:9–16). This essentially restorative approach would eventually be combined with the more apocalyptic in the Dead Sea sect, a matter to which we will return.

Ben Sira (ca. 170 BCE) expresses his hope for a better future in 36:11–17. Nonetheless, here the text speaks only of a return to the ancient glories. No messianic king is mentioned. The continuance of the priesthood is much more prominent than that of the Davidic dynasty (45:24–25). The notion of

⁵ See the summary of J. Licht, "Day of the Lord," *EJ* 5. 1387–88.
⁶ See L. H. Schiffman, "Jewish Sectarianism in Second Temple Times," *Great Schisms in Jewish History* (ed. R. Jospe and S. M. Wagner; New York: Ktav, 1981) 1–46.

Elijah as harbinger of the messiah appears in 48:10–11. An additional prayer in Hebrew in the medieval manuscripts (51:12) describes God as the redeemer of Israel and gatherer of the dispersed, Who builds His city and His holy place and Who causes a horn to sprout from the house of David. These passages, assuming they are indeed part of the original work, would indicate that the restoration of the rule of the Davidic house was a central part of the author's view of the coming redemption.[7]

The *Psalms of Solomon,* composed probably in the time of Pompey (63–48 BCE), give much prominence to the figure of the messianic king. The author emphasizes the kingship of God as well as the permanent nature of the Davidic house (17:1, 5). The Roman domination of Jerusalem in the author's time encouraged his longing for a Davidic king. This king is expected to rule over Israel, crush its enemies, and cleanse Jerusalem of the Gentiles (17:23–27). Righteousness will reign and the land will again be returned to the tribal inheritances (17:28–31). The Gentiles will serve the Davidic king and come up to Jerusalem to see the glory of the Lord. This righteous king will bless his people with wisdom and be blessed by God. He is described as "anointed of the Lord." This messiah, despite God's providential benevolence on his behalf, is seen as a worldly ruler, a real king of Israel.[8]

Extremely significant but at the same time elusive is the relationship of the Pharisees and the Sadducees to the question of messianic belief. Josephus relates that these two groups were divided over the eternality of the soul which the Pharisees accepted but which the Sadducees did not.[9] This has led some scholars to the unsupported assumption that the Pharisees adopted a belief in the messiah while the Sadducees, holding more literally to biblical tradition, did not expect a future age. This claim is totally unsubstantiated. There is no reason to believe that the Sadducees did not accept the notion of a restorative messianism in accord with the biblical traditions. We cannot speculate on the Pharisaic messianism of this time either. As in so many other matters, the views of the Pharisees and Sadducees must remain shrouded in mystery.

The Second Temple views discussed thus far are essentially restorative. The more utopian view is expressed initially in the book of Daniel and those sources which follow its approach. Most of the later sources combine the Davidic messiah with the motif of the victory of the righteous from Daniel. The book of Daniel expects that a time of deliverance will follow the present age of distress (12:1). God will judge the kingdoms of this world and their

---

[7] E. Schürer, *The History of the Jewish People in the Age of Jesus Christ* (ed. G. Vermes, F. Millar and M. Black; Edinburgh: T. & T. Clark, 1979) 2. 498–500. Messianic concepts as such do not figure in 1 and 2 Maccabees, since they do not look forward to the Davidic restoration. Some eschatological motifs do occur, however. See Schürer, *History*, 2. 500.

[8] Schürer, *History*, 2. 503–5.

[9] Josephus, *J.W.* 2.7.14 §163; *Ant.* 18.1.3 §14; *Ant.* 18.1.4 §16.

powers will be taken away. The "holy ones of the Most High" will inherit eternal dominion. The righteous and the evildoers will both be resurrected to receive their just deserts. Daniel does not seem to have envisaged a messianic king. It appears that the "son of man" should not be taken as a messianic figure. The son of man is rather a representation for the people of the Most High.[10] The ascent of the righteous is a result of their conquest of the evildoers.

Sybilline Oracles 3:652–795, usually dated to ca. 140 BCE, is almost exclusively messianic in content. Yet only at the beginning is the messianic king mentioned briefly. This king will put an end to war, in obedience to God's command. When this king arises, the Gentile kings will attack the temple and the Land of Israel. Yet God will cause them to perish. Various natural phenomena will accompany this process, as in the biblical Day of the Lord. These attackers will die and the children of God will live in peace and tranquillity with God's help. This defeat will cause the Gentiles to return to God's law, and peace will now prevail. God will establish an everlasting kingdom over the earth.[11]

Although the older strata of the Ethiopic *Enoch* (*1 Enoch*) have little messianic material, the vision of the end of history in 90:16–38 is relevant. The author expects a final attack by the Gentiles who will be defeated with God's miraculous intervention. A throne will be erected on which God will sit in judgment. God will then replace the old Jerusalem with a new one. Here the pious Israelites will live and the Gentiles will pay homage to them. The messiah will then appear and all the Gentiles will adopt the ways of the Lord. Here the messiah enters only at the end of a process which God Himself ushers in. The Parables of Enoch (chaps. 37–71) primarily follow the approach of the book of Daniel with one exception. The expression "son of man" is now applied to the messiah. He is assumed literally to come from heaven and to be pre-existent.[12]

The *Assumption of Moses,* written most probably around the turn of the era, mentions no messiah but expresses a wish for the destruction of the wicked (chap. 10). The same vision of the future attends *Jub.* 23:27–31; 32:18–19; 31:18–20. The *Assumption of Moses* speaks of a messianic figure, an angel of God, but no human agent of salvation is mentioned.[13]

---

[10] Mowinckel, *He that Cometh,* 348–53. C. Caragounis (*The Son of Man: Vision and Interpretation* [Tübingen: J. C. B. Mohr, 1986] especially 81) argues that the son of man is a transcendant figure of heavenly nature. Similar is the view of G. R. Beasley-Murray (*Jesus and the Kingdom of God* [Grand Rapids: Eerdmans, 1986], 221).

[11] Schürer, *History,* 2. 501–3.

[12] Schürer, *History,* 2. 502–3. See also G. W. E. Nickelsburg, "Salvation without and with a Messiah: Developing Beliefs in Writings Ascribed to Enoch," *Judaisms and Their Messiahs at the Turn of the Christian Era* (ed. J. Neusner, W. S. Green and E. Frerichs; Cambridge: Cambridge University Press, 1987) 49–68.

[13] Schürer, *History,* 2. 506–7. See also J. J. Collins, "Messianism in the Maccabean Period," *Judaisms and Their Messiahs at the Turn of the Christian Era* (ed. J. Neusner, W. S. Green and

This second group of sources take up the utopian trend, expecting the eventual destruction of all the wicked. They are closely linked to dualistic ideas regarding the struggle between good and evil. Although, as Scholem pointed out, each approach includes elements of the other, it was left for the Qumran sect to bring both trends prominently into one system, thus creating at the same time tremendous tension and tremendous power.

Messianism in the Dead Sea Scrolls

From the very beginning of the study of the Dead Sea Scrolls, it has been clear that the documents of the Qumran sect place great emphasis on eschatology. A number of documents are almost completely dedicated to issues related to the end of days.[14] From the *Scroll of the War of the Sons of Light against the Sons of Darkness*[15] it can be seen that the sect expected to participate in the battle which would usher in the final age. Indeed, as a result of that battle all evildoers would be destroyed, and the sect would remain as the true people of Israel.

This cataclysmic battle and the changes in the world order expected along with it, among other factors, have led many to label the Qumran group apocalyptic. The notion of a great battle, similar in many ways to the Day of the Lord of the Hebrew Bible, does indeed typify apocalyptic sects.[16] The Qumran group was one of many such groups which operated in the Second Commonwealth period. Various other texts from the Qumran corpus, including the 4Q *Florilegium*,[17] have greatly added to our understanding of the messianic age in the ideology of the Qumran sect.

Above, the origins of the two-messiah concept were already noted. According to the Dead Sea Scrolls, these two messiahs were to lead the congregation in the end of days. At the same time the sect expected a prophet who was a quasi-messianic figure. The notion of a priestly messiah fits well with the place of the priesthood in the origins, leadership and organization of the Qumran sect. The messiah of Aaron was expected to be superior and to dominate religious matters, while the messiah of Israel would rule over

E. Frerichs; Cambridge: Cambridge University Press, 1987) 97–109 and J. A. Goldstein, "How the Authors of 1 and 2 Maccabees Treated the 'Messianic' Promises," *Judaisms and Their Messiahs at the Turn of the Christian Era* (ed. J. Neusner, W. S. Green and E. Frerichs; Cambridge: Cambridge University Press, 1987) 69–96.

[14] For a recent survey, see Collins, *Apocalyptic Imagination*, 115–41. See also S. Talmon, "Waiting for the Messiah: The Spiritual Universe of the Qumran Covenanters," *Judaisms and Their Messiahs at the Turn of the Christian Era* (ed. J. Neusner, W. S. Green and E. Frerichs; Cambridge: Cambridge University Press, 1987) 111–37.

[15] Y. Yadin, *The Scroll of the War of the Sons of Light against the Sons of Darkness* (Oxford: Oxford University Press, 1962).

[16] Cf. Collins, *Apocalyptic Imagination*, 1–11.

[17] J. M. Allegro, *Qumrân Cave 4* (Discoveries in the Judaean Desert 5; Oxford: Clarendon Press, 1968) frag. 1–2, I, lines 11–13 (p. 53).

temporal and political matters. Both messiahs would preside over the eschatological banquet. This model is based on the Moses/Aaron, Joshua/ Zerubbabel type of pairing and was represented by Bar Kokhba and the High Priest Eleazar in the Bar Kokhba revolt (132–135 CE) as well. The same approach is found in the *Testaments of the Twelve Patriarchs* where the king from the tribe of Judah is inferior to the messianic priest.[18] Those sectarian texts expecting a single Davidic messiah are of the restorative type, while those expecting two messiahs, a lay messiah (not said to be Davidic) and a priestly messiah, follow the utopian trend.

Thus far we have been describing restorative tendencies based on the biblical prophetic visions. Yet the Qumran sect went much further. Like the apocalyptic trend, it expected that the advent of the messianic age would be heralded by the great war described in *The Scroll of the War of the Sons of Light against the Sons of Darkness*. It would mean the victory of the forces of good over those of evil, in heaven above and on earth below. After forty years the period of wickedness would come to an end; the elect would attain glory. The messianic banquet presided over by the two messiahs, described in the *Rule of the Congregation* (סרך העדה), would usher in the new age which would include worship at the eschatological temple. The sacrificial worship would be conducted according to the law as envisaged by the sectarian leaders. In essence, the messianic vision was to include the reaching of a level of purity and perfection in the observance of Jewish law impossible in the present age. The utopian trend manifests itself here not only in the destruction of the wicked at the end of a great cosmic battle, but also in the sphere of Jewish law. Only in the future age will it be possible properly to observe the Torah as interpreted by the sect.

Equally important is the notion of the immediacy of the *eschaton*. The old order would soon come to an end. The forces of evil and those opposing the sect were soon to be destroyed. The new order had already dawned with the sect's removal to the desert from the main population centers of Judea and the establishment of the sectarian center at Qumran. The sect lived on the verge of the *eschaton*, with one foot, as it were, in the present age and one foot in the future age. The messianic era would happen in their lifetime. Their life in the sect was dedicated to preparing for that new age by living as if it had already come. It is in this framework that we will have to approach the סרך העדה (*Rule of the Congregation*) which forms the subject of this study, for it sets out the nature of the future community of perfect holiness.

We cannot date precisely the elements of Qumran messianic doctrine or their crystallization except to place them sometime in the Hasmonean

---

[18] Cf. J. Liver, "The Doctrine of the Two Messiahs in Sectarian Literature in the Time of the Second Commonwealth," *HTR* 52 (1959) 149–85 and L. H. Schiffman, "Messianic Figures and Ideas in the Qumran Scrolls," to appear in *The Messiah* (ed. J. H. Charlesworth; Anchor Bible Reference Library; Garden City: Doubleday).

period. During this era the sect flourished on the shores of the Dead Sea and composed its texts. The combination of the two trends, restorative and utopian, appearing at Qumran for the first time, later exercised a powerful role in the future of Jewish messianic speculation.

The Rule of the Congregation

Among the most significant documents of eschatological speculation deriving from the Qumran sect is the סרך העדה (1QSa). This text, called in English the *Rule of the Congregation*, is an appendix to the סרך היחד (1QS, the *Manual of Discipline*). The *Rule of the Congregation*, along with the other appendix to the *Manual of Discipline*, the סרך הברכות, known as the *Rule of Benedictions* (1QSb), was unknown when the *Manual of Discipline* was first published in 1951.[19] Subsequently, the two appendixes were discovered among the fragments from cave 1 and were published in 1955.[20] The editors proved beyond a doubt that the *Rule of the Congregation* originally stood immediately after the last column of the *Manual of Discipline* in the manuscript of 1QS.[21]

The מגילת הסרכים (*Rule Scroll*) is now seen as a three-part document including: (1) the *Manual of Discipline* (סרך היחד), (2) the *Rule of the Congregation* (סרך העדה) and (3) the *Rule of Benedictions* (סרך הברכות). Our exemplar of the entire unit of three texts has been dated on palaeographic grounds by F. M. Cross to ca. 100–75 BCE. This manuscript is certainly copied from an earlier *Vorlage*. Milik has identified ten manuscripts of the *Manual of Discipline* from cave 4. This makes it extremely likely that the three texts were composed independently, and that they were joined into the *Rule Scroll* by a scribe who recognized their conceptual unity.

Rule of the Congregation is a messianic document picturing the ideal constitution of the sect in the end of days. The text is based upon the same theological and doctrinal presuppositions as is the *Manual of Discipline*. It begins with a brief introduction outlining its purposes and then describes the members of the community according to the functions they assume at

---

[19] M. Burrows, with J. C. Trever and W. H. Brownlee, *The Dead Sea Scrolls of Saint Mark's Monastery*, Volume 2, Fascicle 2 (New Haven: American Schools of Oriental Research, 1951).

[20] D. Barthélemy and J. T. Milik, *Qumran Cave I*, Discoveries in the Judaean Desert (Oxford: Clarendon Press, 1955) 1. 107–30. Subsequent commentaries referred to below are those of H. N. Richardson, "Some Notes on 1QSa," *JBL* 76 (1957) 108–22; J. Carmignac, "La règle de la congrégation," *Les textes de Qumran* (ed. J. Carmignac, É. Cothenet and H. Lignée; Paris: Letouzey et Ané, 1963) 2. 11–27; J. Maier, *Die Texte vom Toten Meer* (Munich and Basel: Ernst Reinhardt, 1960) 2. 154–61, and J. Licht, מגילת הסרכים (Jerusalem: Mosad Bialik, 1965) 241–70. A few notes are found in E. Lohse, *Die Texte aus Qumran* (Munich: Kösel-Verlag, 1986) 286.

[21] Cf. M. Martin, *The Scribal Character of the Dead Sea Scrolls* (Louvain: Institut Orientaliste, 1958) 1. 49–56; R. North, "Qumran 'Serek a' and Related Fragments," *Orientalia* N.S. 25 (1956) 90–99.

various stages in their lives. It next pictures an eschatological meeting of the מושב הרבים, the sectarian assembly[22] (although this term is not used), emphasizing the ritual purity of the group and the exclusion from it of those afflicted with physical blemishes and imperfections. Finally, the text describes a banquet at the end of days at which the two messianic figures expected by the sect will preside.[23] The events predicted in this text actually constitute a kind of messianic mirror image of the society described in the *Manual of Discipline*. After all, the sect saw itself as living on the verge of the end of days and must have attempted to realize in the sectarian life of the *Manual* the very same level of perfection and purity which was to characterize the future age. The community described in the *Manual* is an attempt to create messianic conditions, even before the coming of the *eschaton*, and to realize the sectarians' dreams of the future in the present.

This conclusion will also be central from a methodological point of view. It will allow us to assume that legal materials contained in the *Rule of the Congregation* were actualized in the everyday life of the sect. This suggestion has been borne out in our work time and again where parallel texts exist, and it allows us to reconstruct various aspects of sectarian doctrine for both the present and future ages.

Most importantly, we will see in this study how the sect looked forward to an era of absolute purity and perfection. The onset of the messianic age would allow the sectarians to fulfill their utopian dreams and aspirations which could not be fully realized in this world. The sect's councils would be free of all ritual impurity and only those who were physically perfect would be admitted to them. The culmination of the messianic yearnings of the Qumranites would come in the messianic banquet presided over by the two messiahs. This banquet was of such great importance that the sectarians regularly ate communal meals in the present age in expectation of it, and archaeological remains of the kitchen, ovens, crockery and deposits of animal bones all testify to the importance of this notion.

The Method of the Study

The materials under study here differ somewhat from those we have examined previously. Whereas our earlier studies have dealt with material analogous to what the later rabbis termed *halakhah*, loosely translated as "Jewish law," our study of the *Rule of the Congregation* must place greater

---

[22] On the מושב הרבים, see L. H. Schiffman, *The Halakhah at Qumran* (Leiden: E. J. Brill, 1975) 68–70.

[23] Cf. Licht, מגילת הסרכים, 241–49 and Carmignac, "La règle," 11–14 for general introductions to the text. For a survey of materials relating to purity at Qumran, see M. Newton, *The Concept of Purity at Qumran and in the Letters of Paul* (Cambridge: Cambridge University Press, 1985) 1–51.

emphasis on sectarian doctrines as well. For this reason, the method of this study is somewhat different from that of our previous works.

Nonetheless, it is based, like the earlier volumes, first and foremost on close philological and historical study. Each text must be understood initially as an individual, discrete passage and then placed in the framework of the document in which it is found, and, finally, in the Qumran corpus as a whole. Each passage must then be compared with other Jewish texts and traditions from contemporary Second Temple sources or from the somewhat later tannaitic corpus in order to provide a wider background for its exegesis.

First, the correct text must be fixed as accurately as possible, based on examination of photographs of the manuscript and the various reconstructions and emendations proposed. For the most part, the readings and reconstructions of J. Licht have been accepted, although not without exception. Detailed philological notes were prepared, dealing with the relationship of the text to biblical citations, other Qumran texts, and such issues as grammar and lexicography. Over and over it was found that through preparing these notes the correct interpretation of the text became apparent. Without such examination, we would simply be guessing at the true significance of the material.

Individual passages must be looked at in the context of the document as a whole. This study presents an analysis of the entire *Rule of the Congregation* in order. Nevertheless, the structure of a commentary has been avoided at all costs. Such an approach would have prevented the explication of the relevance of this text to the corpus of Qumran literature as a whole and the placing of its various aspects within the framework of the history of messianism and religious law in Israel. This approach has yielded somewhat of a cross between a collection of studies and a commentary. It is hoped that this means of exposition will provide the clearest view of this text. In the conclusions, we attempt to tie together the various threads which run through this study and to place them in the context of the ideology and law of the sect and the history of Jewish eschatology.

Our previous studies have been for the most part legal, as already noted. In this text, the *Rule of the Congregation*, we see the merging of the concepts of law and messianism. This study deals with a system of practice and ritual which expresses the very foundations of the eschatological beliefs of the sect. If the ultimate perfection was to be achieved in the end of days, then the life of the sectarian in this world would have to be an imitation, however pale, of those ideals. Like all Jewish groups of the Second Commonwealth, the sectarians of Qumran dreamed of a better future, one which would make possible the proper observance of the law as they interpreted it, one which would strengthen the bond between the Israelites and their Creator and Lawgiver, a life of purity and perfection.

1

THE ESCHATOLOGICAL COMMUNITY
AND THE STAGES OF SECTARIAN LIFE

Introduction to the Text

1QSa 1:1–5 contains a short introduction indicating the purpose of the text. This passage begins with an introductory rubric and a more extensive definition follows:[1]

וזה הסרך לכול עדת ישראל באחרית הימים: בהספם ליחד להתהלך על פי
משפט בני צדוק הכוהנים ואנושי בריתם אשר סרו מלכת בדרך העם.
המה אנושי עצתו אשר שמרו בריתו בתוך רשעה לכנפר בעד הארץ].
בבואם יקהילו את כול הבאים מטף עד נשים וקראו באוזניהם] את [כול
חוקי הברית ולהבינם בכול משפטיה]מה פן ישגו במנ]שוגותיהמה].

And this is the rule[2] for all of the congregation of Israel in the end of days:
When they assem[ble[3] as a community[4] to li]ve according to the regulation
of the Sons of Zadok, the priests,[5] and the men of their covenant who have
[turned away from living in the w]ay of the people.[6] These are the people
of His (God's) counsel who have kept their covenant with Him[7] amidst the
evil to a[tone for the land.][8] When they come, they shall assemble[9] all those

---

[1] Most restorations of 1QSa are according to Licht. For others see the commentaries discussed above, 8, n. 20.

[2] See L. H. Schiffman, *The Halakhah at Qumran* (Leiden: E. J. Brill, 1975) 60–68.

[3] The root is אסף, with the א assimilated. This form is common in Qumran Hebrew.

[4] This translation conforms to the Qumran usage of יחד as a substantive denoting the Qumran community. It is also possible to translate: "When they assemble together."

[5] Cf. Schiffman (*Halakhah at Qumran,* 72–76) on the role of the Zadokite priests in Qumran literature and the Bible.

[6] Cf. Licht (מגילת הסרכים [Jerusalem: Mosad Bialik, 1965] 252), who notes the close parallel in 4QFlorilegium 1:14–16. The use of עם, "people," here is similar to the tannaitic use of עם הארץ, "people of the land," for those Jews not part of the group or sect.

[7] Or "His covenant."

[8] Cf. Num 35:33 and Deut 32:43. J. Maier (*Texte vom Toten Meer* [Munich and Basel: Ernst Reinhardt, 1960] 2. 154) observes that the sect is seen as providing atonement which the defiled Jerusalem temple can no longer provide.

[9] The הפעיל of קהל with the object עדה occurs in Exod 35:1; Lev 8:3; Num 1:18; 8:9; 16:19; and 20:8. The use of this expression is limited to descriptions of the desert-wandering period. This period was extremely important to the sect's self-image, as shown in S. Talmon, "The 'Desert Motif' in the Bible and in Qumran Literature," *Biblical Motifs* (ed. A. Altmann; Cambridge: Harvard University Press, 1966) 31–63.

who join,[10] women and children, and they shall read to [them[11] all] the laws of the covenant and instruct them in all their regu[lations] lest they err in their [mistakes].

This text defines the basic intent of the *Rule of the Congregation*, namely, to describe the nature of the congregation in the end of days. The entire community of Israel is to be identical with the sect in the end of days. The enemies of the sect would perish in the final battle described in the *War Scroll*. All those destined to join the Sons of Light would do so as the *eschaton* dawned. All others would be destroyed. The sect, in its newly expanded form, would now constitute the entirety of the Congregation of Israel.[12] In the end of days, as in the present state of affairs, the sect would be led by "the Sons of Zadok, the priests, and the men of their counsel." This requirement is repeated again and again in the sectarian texts. Yet it has been suggested that this role became largely ceremonial as time progressed.[13] Indeed, some texts even define the entire sect as the Sons of Zadok.[14] On the other hand, we can expect that the eschatological priest (הכוהן) would certainly be of the Zadokite lineage. Even in the end of days, then, just as in the present age, the sect would be dominated, even if only formally, by the Zadokite priesthood.

The Zadokites and the members of the sect are seen as having forsworn the improper conduct of the rest of the people (העם). The self-image of the sect in the present age is here repeated. Indeed, we can see from this passage that even though the sect believed that it alone would inherit the end of days, it assumed that it would continue to see itself as the persecuted (or once persecuted) minority. After all, despite the evil that surrounded them, the sectarians had persevered.

Yet another important aspect of their self-definition in the present is illuminated here. We are told that through its adherence to its covenant with God, the sect had atoned for the land. Had the sect not held fast to the correct interpretation of the law, the land would have suffered complete destruction at the hands of God. The sect's law included both the "revealed" (נגלה), commandments clearly explained in the Torah, and the "hidden" (נסתר), those commandments the correct interpretation of which could only be discovered by inspired biblical exegesis and which were known only to the initiates of the sect.[15] The sect's observance of the law prevented the

----

[10] On בוא as a term for joining the sect, see S. Lieberman, "The Discipline in the So-called Dead Sea Manual of Discipline," *JBL* 71 (1951) 202.

[11] Literally, "in their ears," *i.e.* "hearing."

[12] Cf. J. Licht, "מטעת עולם ועם פדות אל," מחקרים במגילות הגנוזות (ed. Y. Yadin and C. Rabin; Jerusalem: Hekhal Ha-Sefer, 1961) 49–75.

[13] Cf. L. H. Schiffman, *Sectarian Law in the Dead Sea Scrolls, Courts, Testimony and the Penal Code* (Chico: Scholars Press, 1983) 5.

[14] CD 4:3–4; 9:14, where, however, MS d has הצדק.

[15] For these legal categories, see Schiffman, *Halakhah at Qumran*, 22–32.

destruction of the Jewish people who were otherwise deserving of so grievous a penalty.

As the *eschaton* dawns, the sectarians are to assemble together, as a newly expanded community, now constituting the only Israel. This assemblage, like the biblical assemblages that came before, would constitute a covenant renewal ceremony on the analogy of what the rabbis termed הקהל. Not only would adult, male members of the sect attend, but women and children would join as well. This is in conformity with the prescriptions of Deuteronomy 29 that also influenced other passages of the Dead Sea corpus.[16] This covenant renewal ceremony, like those described in the Bible,[17] would be an opportunity for the teaching of the Torah and its regulations. Since the term משפטים denotes the law as derived by the sectarian system of biblical exegesis,[18] we can safely conclude that the purpose of this ceremony will be much more than simply teaching the written Scriptures of the Jewish people. This occasion would entail the detailed instruction of the many new sectarians (if we can term the only Israel "the sect") in the true interpretations of the Qumran community. This would now be the only pattern of Jewish observance. It is certainly to be assumed that this instruction would have been part of a process similar to that used to induct new sectarians in the present age. It would involve a series of stages in which the new member was gradually inducted into the principles and teachings of the sect. As the initiate advanced, he would be considered to be less impure, and would be included as well in the communal meals of the sect, meals that in the present age are themselves anticipations of the dawning of the long-awaited and earnestly hoped for *eschaton*.[19]

The List of Ages

The *Rule of the Congregation* next provides a detailed list of various ages and of the duties and privileges of members who attain these specified stages of life. At the end of this section there is also discussion of the disqualified as well as of the status of the Levites. The heading of the passage reads (1QSa 1:6):

וזה הסרך לכול צבאות העדה לכול האזרח בישראל: . . .

This is the rule for all the hosts of the congregation, for every native-born in Israel: . . .

The importance of this heading for our purposes is in its terminology. Once

---

[16] Cf. 1QS 2:13–17.

[17] For such assemblies, see Deuteronomy 29–31; Joshua 24; 2 Kings 23; and Nehemiah 9–10.

[18] See Schiffman, *Halakhah at Qumran*, 42–47.

[19] See Schiffman, *Sectarian Law*, 161–65 on admission to the sect. Communal meals are taken up below in Chapter Four.

again we encounter familiar sectarian images. The sect itself is described as צבאות העדה, "the hosts of the congregation." This phrase is made up of two terms recalling the desert period in Israel's history. While originally a military term, צבאות is appropriate for the Qumran community, as it was for Israel in the desert, precisely because both communities were organized along military lines, with officers of tens, fifties, hundreds and thousands. At Qumran, regular mustering ceremonies took place, and they were to be part of the eschatalogical war of the *War Scroll*.[20] The very same imagery is in evidence in the use of the term אזרח ("citizen") used elsewhere for the native-born Jew in the desert period.

Early Childhood

At this point the text turns to a description of the first stage in life, the years of childhood, extending up to the age of ten (1QSa 1:6–8):

ומן נעוריו ילמ[ד]הו בספר ההגי וכפי יומיו ישכיליהו בחוק[ין] הברית ו[לפי
שכלו יי[ס]רו במשפטיהמה.

From his yo[uth they[21] shall instru]ct him in the Book of Hagi/u, and according to his age they[22] shall enlighten him in the law[s of] the covenant.[23] [And according to his understanding they shall] teach him their regulations.

That the sect would have assumed that there was an obligation to instruct children in the teachings of the Torah is in line with what we know of the history of Jewish education. Jewish schools were already widespread in the Hellenistic period.[24] Those at Qumran must have been very much on the pattern of the old priestly schools, considering the priestly role in the conduct of sectarian affairs. The eschatological description in our text probably reflects the realities of the sectarian community in the Judaean desert. Our text tells us that entrance to these schools would be at an early age, sometime before the age of ten. The Bible uses the very same phrase,

---

[20] See Y. Yadin, *The Scroll of the War of the Sons of Light Against the Sons of Darkness* (Oxford: Oxford University Press, 1962) 49–53, 59–60.

[21] This most probably refers to the teachers of the sect who are enjoined to instruct the children. It might also be an impersonal usage, tantamount to a passive, meaning "he shall be instructed." Barthélemy restores וללמ[ד]הו] (D. Barthélemy and J. T. Milik, *Qumran Cave I, Discoveries in the Judaean Desert 1* [Oxford: Clarendon Press, 1955] 109).

[22] Perhaps read ישכילוהו.

[23] Cf. line 5 for the same phrase. There it was substituted for the biblical התורה הזאת of Deut 31:12. It also appears in CD 20:29. ברית in the Qumran texts describes not only the special relationship between God and Israel, but also that into which the sectarians have entered together to actualize that relationship.

[24] See E. Schürer, *The History of the Jewish People in the Age of Jesus Christ* (Edinburgh: T. & T. Clark, 1979) 2. 415–22 and the bibliography cited there.

מנעוריו, to refer to early youth.[25] Job 31:18 shows that this phrase can denote earliest childhood. From comparison with tannaitic evidence, we can conclude that early learning must have begun in the family setting, with actual schooling starting at six or seven.[26]

Our passage tells us about the curriculum of the young pupil. He is to study the ספר ההגי/ו from his earliest youth. This term has been shown on linguistic and contextual grounds to refer to the Torah.[27] Our passage supports this conclusion since Jewish schools of this period began earliest instruction with the Torah.[28]

According to his age, the pupil would also be taught the חוקין הברית, "the laws of the covenant." This phrase probably refers to the practical application of the commandments. Indeed, this concept is described in rabbinic usage as חינוך, initiation into the observance of the commandments. At various stages the child was introduced to the observance of specific commandments so as to ease the eventual transition to a full role in Jewish life.

Finally, and in accord with his demonstrated aptitudes and progress, the young boy would be taught the sectarian regulations, believed by the sect to be the result of inspired biblical exegesis. These teachings are reserved for a later stage than that at which the teaching of the Torah and the commandments is introduced. The method is likewise paralleled in tannaitic usage in which the extrabiblical traditions of the rabbis, the oral law in the form of the Mishnah, are reserved for a later age than is the teaching of Scripture.[29]

The Age of Ten

The text now introduces the minimum age of ten with an enigmatic statement (1QSa 1:8):

עשר שנים יבוא בטף.

For ten years he shall be enumerated[30] among the children.[31]

---

[25] BDB, 654–55, s.v. נער.

[26] For a collection of rabbinic material, see N. Drazin, A History of Jewish Education (Baltimore: Johns Hopkins Press, 1940).

[27] See Schiffman, Halakhah at Qumran, 44 n. 144. Note that our text has ההגי while other occurrences have ההגו. It is possible, as noted by Licht, to emend to ההגו in our passage and to assume confusion of the ו and י in some Vorlage. After all, these letters are virtually identical in most Qumran MSS.

[28] Drazin (History, 82–83) shows that there is no evidence from tannaitic sources for the teaching of Leviticus as the pupil's introduction to the Torah.

[29] See m. 'Abot 5:21.

[30] For this use of כוא see 1 Chr 4:38 (cf. BDB, 98).

[31] Barthélemy reads בטב (DJD 1. 109), and is followed by H. N. Richardson, "Some Notes on 1QSa," JBL 76 (1957) 111. Barthélemy's own translation, et qu'il progresse (DJD 1. 112), makes his reading quite improbable. His dismissal of the reading טף in light of the poor state of the correction of the MS is unnecessary. It is unlikely that this ten year period is to be related to

It is not clear from the text as it stands whether the status of טף is to be assigned to the child from birth until the tenth year or from the tenth year until the twentieth. Licht conjectures that the status of טף is in effect for the first ten years of the life of the sectarian after which he enters the status of נער, which does not appear in our text.[32] This is indeed a possibility. On the other hand, it is also possible that the statement immediately preceding, dealing with the early education of the child, refers to the first ten years, with the status of טף applying to the next ten years. In this case, the text would be complete as it stands.

While no definitive answer to this question can be proposed, it is certainly true that comparison with the tannaitic exegesis of the biblical term טף would support the view that Licht proposed. To the tannaim, the טף were children below the age at which they could even understand the commandments and make moral choices. They lacked the "knowledge of good and evil," a matter to which we shall shortly return. Because they were still too young to come on their own, such children had to be brought to the covenant ceremony (הקהל) by their parents.[33]

The Age of Twenty

Our text now discusses the age of twenty, that was, in fact, the age of legal majority in Qumran sources. Accordingly, 1QSa 1:9–11 provides:

ובן עשרים שנה יעבור על הפקודים לבוא בגורל בתוך משפחׄתׄו ליחד
בעׄדׄתׄן קׄדׄש. ולׄוׄא יׄקרבׄן אׄלׄן אשה לדעתה למשכבי זכר כי אם לפי מולואת
לו עשׄרׄים שׄנה בדעתו [טובן ורע.

> And at twenty year[s of age he shall pass among the mu]stered to enter into full status along with his fam[il]y, to join the holy congre[gation].[34] He shall not [approach] a woman to have sexual relations with her until he reaches the age of twe[nty] years at which time he knows [good] and evil.[35]

This text clearly establishes twenty as the age for mustering. This mustering, however, was not the military conscription that was to begin at age twenty-five. Rather, it was the minimum age for full-fledged membership in the sect and included the rights of testimony, voting in the assembly, and marriage.

---

the ten years of membership in the sect alluded to in 1QS 7:22–25, on which see Schiffman, *Sectarian Law*, 168–69.

[32] Note that 1QM 7:3 describes those below military age (twenty-five) as נער זעטוט. Cf. Yadin, *War Scroll*, 290.

[33] *Mekhilta' De-Rabbi Ishmael, Bo'* 16 (ed. H. S. Horovitz and I. A. Rabin; Jerusalem: Bamberger and Wahrmann, 1960, p. 59), *t. Sota* 7:9. Below we will see that the sect took the knowledge of good and evil as referring to sexual awareness and assumed that such maturity arrived at twenty.

[34] For detailed philological commentary, see Schiffman, *Sectarian Law*, 67–68, nn. 19–23.

[35] See Schiffman, *Sectarian Law*, 70, nn. 65–69; Maier, *Texte*, 2. 155.

The conferral of rights of membership in the sect is also indicated in CD 15:5–6:

והבא בברית לכול ישראל לחוק עולם את בניהם אשר יגיעו לעבור על
הפקודים בשבועת הברית יקימו עליהם.

And as to anyone who enters the covenant from among all Israel, as an eternal ordinance,[36] their sons who reach the age of passing among the mustered shall take upon themselves the oath of the covenant.[37]

Here the son of a member of the sect attains the age of mustering and takes upon himself the oath of allegiance to the sectarian laws and the sectarian interpretation of the Torah. He is no longer regarded as the child of a member but as a member of the sect himself.

This oath of the covenant was probably only incumbent upon the males of the sect. Their wives and daughters were members of the sect by virtue of the status of their male relatives. This procedure can be compared to the biblical regulations governing the distribution of priestly dues (Num 18:11–12, 25–32). The entire household of the priest was permitted to eat of the תרומות.

As long as a girl lived in her father's house, she was permitted to partake of these dues. However, if she married a non-priest, she no longer retained these rights. It was possible for her to regain these rights if she had no children and was divorced or widowed and returned to her father's house (Lev 22:10–14). The laws governing the utilization of תרומות are particularly appropriate for understanding the Qumran text, for it is known that the sectarians attempted to maintain in their everyday meals the ritual purity which the priests observed while eating תרומות.

The חבורה described in tannaitic sources also regarded the purity laws as vital to its way of life. Tannaitic הלכה regarding the חבורה also expects the status of the family of the member (חבר) to derive from the male head of the household. A man who became a member of the חבורה by accepting the regulations of the group before a court of three of its members[38] then represented the חבורה in swearing in his family. Children born after he became a חבר automatically belonged to the חבורה.[39] Women who married into the חבורה had to be specially accepted, however.[40] Whereas the sect

---

[36] That is, the process is to be repeated generation after generation.

[37] Cf. CD 15:6–11, 1QS 6:13–15.

[38] See t. Dem. 2:14 (and S. Lieberman, תוספתא כפשוטה [New York: Jewish Theological Seminary, 1955] 1. 216–17) which mentions the full חבורה, and a ברייתא in b. Bek. 30b which mentions the three representatives. Lieberman ("Discipline," 200, n. 15) assumes that the Babylonian recension is secondary and that the acceptance of חברות took place before the entire חבורה. A. Oppenheimer (The 'Am Ha-'Aretz [Leiden: E. J. Brill, 1977], 120, n. 7) takes this variation as the result of differing practices or date.

[39] Y. Dem. 2:3 (23a); Lieberman, תוספתא כפשוטה, 1. 216–17.

[40] T. Dem. 2:16 and Lieberman, תוספתא כפשוטה, 1. 218. Cf. Oppenheimer, 'Am Ha-'Aretz,

required minors who came of age to take an oath to follow the laws of the sect, the חבורה of tannaitic sources required a public acceptance of its regulations.

The phrase בתוך משפחתו, "along with his family," in our text from the *Rule of the Congregation* is susceptible to two interpretations. Since 1QSa 1:10–11 indicates that twenty is the minimum age for marriage and starting a family, it may be understood that the young man remains under the authority of his family—although he is an independent member of the sect—until he marries and sets up his own household.

A more probable interpretation grants the twenty-year-old full status in the sect along with any members who might be produced by his imminent marriage—his wife and future children. Thus, even a woman not born into the sect can attain the status of a sectarian automatically upon marriage to this member without the steps of the novitiate.

According to 4QOrdinances 2:6–9 it was at this time that the sectarian was to contribute the half shekel:

כסף הנע]רכים אשר נתנו, איש כפר נפשו, מחצית [השקל תרומה לאדנין],
רק [פעם] אחת יתננו כל ימיו.

As to the money of [val]uation which they gave, each as an atonement for himself, a half [shekel as an offering to the Lord,] he shall give it only one [time] in his entire lifetime.

The sect understood that the half shekel of Exod 30:11–16 was to be given only once on the occasion of the first mustering at age twenty.[41]

Our passage from the *Rule of the Congregation* continues:[42]

ובכן תקבל להעיד עליו משפטות התורא ולהתי]צב במשמע משפטים.

And at that time she will be received to bear witness of him (concerning) the judgment of the law and to take (her) pl[a]ce in proclaiming the ordinances.

This sudden shift from the masculine to the feminine and its implication of women's participation in the judicial process has caused some scholars to be suspicious of this passage as it now stands. After all, the context clearly refers to males. It is also difficult to understand why a wife's acceptability as a witness should be connected with that of her husband. Finally, it is unlikely that women were entrusted with assuring the faithfulness of their husbands

---

139 and R. Sarason, *A History of the Mishnaic Law of Agriculture*, Part 3 (Leiden: E. J. Brill, 1979) 1. 90–94.

[41] J. Liver, "מחצית השקל במגילות מדבר יהודה," *Tarbiz* 31 (1960/61) 18–22. Cf. his "פרשת מחצית השקל," *Y. Kaufmann Jubilee Volume* (ed. M. Haran; Jerusalem: Magnes Press, 1960/61) 54–67.

[42] Translated by Richardson, "Notes," 113.

to the sectarian way of life. Therefore, J. M. Baumgarten has emended תקבל
to יקבל and על פי עליו to על פי and translates:[43]

And he shall be received to testify in accordance with the laws of the Torah
and to take [his] place in hearing the judgments.

According to him, the passage wishes to indicate that twenty is the minimum
age for a man to be allowed to attend hearings in court.[44] This emendation
provides the best solution to the difficulties posed by this text.

The age of twenty plays a major role in Jewish legal sources. Tannaitic
הלכה assumed that puberty took place somewhere between the age of
thirteen (for males) or twelve (for females) and twenty. Along with puberty
went the obligation to observe all the commandments. Therefore, while the
age of twenty was definitely binding as the maximum, twelve or thirteen
served as the minimum age. Requiring that obligations be undertaken immediately after the twelfth or thirteenth birthday would ensure that no one who
had possibly passed the age of puberty was not observing all the commandments.[45]

Ezra 3:8 specifies that Levitical service is to begin at twenty. Rabbi
Judah the Prince therefore required a minimum age of twenty for partaking
of sacrifices (קדשי מזבח), serving as precentor, and reciting the priestly
blessing.[46] Several amoraic passages suggest that the heavenly court does not
punish anyone below the age of twenty in order to give the benefit of the
doubt.[47]

The book of *Jubilees* 49:17 and 11QTemple 17:8 both regard the obligation to eat of the paschal lamb as beginning at age twenty.[48] Rabbinic law, however, allowed a child to eat of the paschal lamb provided that he or she could
eat the minimum amount required.[49] *B. Ḥul.* 24b reports that temple priests

[43] "On the Testimony of Women in 1QSa," *JBL* 76 (1957) 266–69, reprinted in his *Studies in
Qumran Law* (Leiden: E. J. Brill, 1977) 183–86. For a summary of the reasoning behind his
emendation and translation of this passage, see Schiffman, *Sectarian Law*, 62–63. Maier, *Texte*,
2. 155–56 follows Baumgarten.

[44] In *m. Sanh.* 4:4 the students of the sages are permitted to observe the proceedings of the
Sanhedrin.

[45] For a full discussion, see Schiffman, *Sectarian Law*, 58–59.

[46] *T. Ḥag.* 1:3 and Lieberman, תוספתא כפשוטה, 5. 1272–76.

[47] *Y. Bik.* 2:1 (64c); *y. Sanh.* 11:7 (30b); *b. Sabb* 89b. Cf. *Gen. Rab.* 58:1 and תוספות יום טוב
to *m. Nid.* 5:9.

[48] See Y. Yadin, *The Temple Scroll* (Jerusalem: Israel Exploration Society, 1983) 2. 74 and the
introductory remarks in 1. 97. Cf. L. H. Schiffman, "The Sacrificial System of the *Temple Scroll*
and the Book of Jubilees," *Society of Biblical Literature 1985 Seminar Papers* (ed. K. H. Richards;
Atlanta: Scholars Press, 1985) 225. 11QTemple 57:2–3 specifies twenty as the minimum age for
military service. Cf. L. H. Schiffman, "The Laws of War in the Temple Scroll," *Mémorial Jean
Carmignac*, ed. F. García Martinez and É. Puech, *RQ* 13 (1988) 300–302.

[49] *T. Ḥag.* 1:2; *b. Sukk.* 42b.

limited their ranks to those who had passed their twentieth birthday. *Y. San.* 4:7 (4:9, 22b) requires the age of judges in capital cases to be at least twenty.[50]

The Age of Twenty-Five

1QSa 1:12–13 mandates that:

ובן חמש ועשׂ֯רים שנה יבוא להתיצ֯ב ביסודות עדת הקודש לעבוד את עבודת העד֯ה].

At twen[ty]-five years of age he will come to take his sta[n]d among the units of the holy congregation to perform the service of the congrega[tion].

Since the age of participation in the mustering ceremony was already specified as twenty (1QSa 1:9–10), it is likely that here we are dealing with the minimum age for military service. This suggestion is confirmed by a parallel in 1QM 7:2–3, dealing with the youngest of the soldiers.

כל מפשיטי החללים ושוללי השלל ומטהרי הארץ ושומרי הכלים ועורך הצידה, כולם יהיו מבן חמש ועשרים שנה ועד בן שלושים.

All those that despoil the slain and collect the booty and cleanse the land and guard the arms and he who prepares the provisions, all these shall be from twenty-five to thirty years old.[51]

Having organized themselves as for the final battle against the Sons of Darkness, the sectarians determined that the age of judging was the same as that of military conscription. Evidence regarding twenty-five as the minimum age for judges comes from CD 10:4–10:

וזה סרך לשפטי העדה . . . מבני חמשה ועשרים שנה עד בן ששים שנה.

And this is the rule for the judges of the congregation . . . from twenty-five years old to sixty years old.

It still remains for us to determine how the sect arrived at the minimum age of twenty-five. The Zadokite priesthood was not only representative of the leaders of the sect but by metonymy often became a term for the sect as a whole. The sectarians attempted to extend the requirements of the priesthood to all members of the group. The regulation of Num 8:24 specifying the minimum age for Levitical service as twenty-five served as the sectarian rule for both military and judicial service. The elevation of all members to this status would ensure the purity of the courts and military camps. This age requirement would be observed both in the pre-messianic period and in the ideal community of the future age.

[50] L. Ginzberg (*An Unknown Jewish Sect* [New York: Jewish Theological Seminary, 1971] 46) finds evidence of a similar rule in the writings of Anan ben David. Cf. Schiffman, *Sectarian Law*, 60.

[51] Trans. in Yadin, *The War Scroll*, 290.

The Age of Thirty

The system of age-limits indicates a minimum age of thirty for service as an officer or official of the sect as seen in 1QSa 1:14–18:

ובן שלושים שנה יגש לריב ריב [ומשפ]ט ולהתיצב ברואשי אלפי ישראל,
לשרי מאות שרי חמ[ש]ים [ו]שרי עשרות, שופטים ושוטרים לשבטיהם,
בכול משפחותם, [ע]ל פ[י] בני [אהר]ן הכוהנים וכול רוש[ין] אבות העדה.
אשר יצא הגורל להתי[נ]צב בע[ב]ודתו [ול]צאת[ן] ולבוא לפני העדה. ולפי שכלו עם
תום דרכו, יחזק מתנו למעמו[ד] לצב[ו]את עבודת מעשו בתוך אחיו. [בין ר]וב
למועט יכבדו איש מרעהו.

At thirty years of age he shall draw near to struggle for the cause of [justi]ce and to take his stand at the head of the thousands of Israel,[52] as officers of hundreds, officers of fi[f]ties, [and officers] of tens,[53] as judges and provosts for their tribes,[54] in all their families, [according t]o the Sons of [Aar]on, the priests, and all the head[s][55] of the clans of the congregation. According to everything which will be decided,[56] he shall take his st[and in (fulfilling) his se]rvice [to go forth] and to come in[57] before the congregation. And according to his understanding along with the perfection of his way, he shall strengthen his loin(s)[58] to take (his) posit[ion to perform [his service][59] among his brothers. [Whether im]portant or unimportant, [one to] another, each shall honor his fellow.

The text here specifies the role of the thirty-year old in the eschatological community. He is to take his rightful place among those eligible to serve in the various official capacities of the congregation. His place in the hierarchy of officials will be determined by the Aaronide priests and the heads of the clans on the basis of his understanding of the teachings of the sect and his attainment of perfection in his way of life.

The age of thirty occurs in several other contexts in sectarian literature. According to CD 14:6–7:

והכהן אשר יפקד את[60] הרבים מבן שלושים שנה עד בן ששים.

---

[52] Cf. Num 11:16 and Josh 22:21.

[53] See 1QSa 1:29–2:1 for a similar sequence. Cf. Exod 18:21; Deut 1:15.

[54] Deut 16:18. The transition to שופטים from שרים was made in accord with Exod 18:22 and Deut 1:16 (in which שוטרים are also mentioned).

[55] Reading [רוש[ין (see Licht, מגילת הסרכים, 258).

[56] Literally, "as the lot goes forth."

[57] Num 27:17; cf. 2 Sam 5:2.

[58] Cf. Nah 2:2.

[59] Cf. Num 8:24, although there the expression refers to the age of twenty-five.

[60] Reading את with S. Schechter, Documents of Jewish Sectaries, Volume I, Fragments of a Zadokite Work (New York: Ktav, 1970) LIII (85). Rabin's restoration to בראש, based on 1QS 6:14, is no more convincing, and, as he indicates, "excludes the otherwise attractive rendering 'who musters'" (C. Rabin, The Zadokite Documents [Oxford: Oxford University Press, 1954] 69). את is used regularly in CD. Cf. E. Y. Kutscher, הלשון והרקע הלשוני של מגילת ישעיהו השלמה

> And the priest who shall muster the assembly (shall be) from thirty to sixty years old.

This passage is in full agreement with the eschatological description. Officials in the present must conform to the same minimum age requirements that we have observed for the age to come.

CD 14:8–9 prescribes the same requirement for the מבקר ("examiner"):[61]

והמבקר אשר לכל המחנות מבן שלושים שנה עד בן חמישים שנה.

> And the examiner of the camps[62] (shall be) from thirty years old to fifty years old.

This official, active as we know in both the legal and financial affairs of the sect, as well as in the implementation of its charitable welfare system, was also required to be at least thirty years old.

What is probably much more important for our purposes is the requirement of the *War Scroll* that the combat troops be at least thirty years old. Speaking about the cavalry, the youngest fighting men, 1QM 6:12–13 states:

והרוכבים עליהם אנשי חיל למלחמה, מלומדי רכב, ותכון ימיהם מבן
שלושים שנה עד בן חמש וארבעים.

> Their riders shall be men of valor for battle, trained in horsemanship, the measure of their age being from thirty to forty-five years.[63]

Yadin has analyzed this requirement of the *War Scroll* in detail. He maintains that this decision was based on the rules of Levitical service. Num 4:3, 23, 30, 35, 39, and 47 would seem, as noted by Yadin, to prescribe an age of thirty for Levitical service. On the other hand, Num 8:24 prescribes a minimum age of twenty-five for such service, as has been noted. The tannaim resolved this contradiction by explaining that from twenty-five the Levite was in training, and that he would enter full service only at thirty.[64] Such an explanation would fit the sect's military organization as well. Even though one began to serve from the age of twenty-five, this service was, in the words of Yadin, as "service troops" who "despoil the slain, collect the booty, cleanse the land, guard the arms, prepare the provisions." Only above the age of thirty did one enter actual combat.[65]

ממגילות ים המלח (Jerusalem: Magnes Press, 1959) 316 and G. W. Nebe, "Der Gebrauch der sogennanten nota accusativi את in Damaskusschrift XV, 5.9 und 12," *RQ* 8 (1973) 257–64.

[61] On this official, see Schiffman, *Sectarian Law*, 37–38, 95–96.

[62] These are the settlements of the sect scattered throughout the country.

[63] Trans. in Yadin, *War Scroll*, 288.

[64] *T. Sheq.* 3:26, *Sifre Be-Midbar* 62 (ed. H. S. Horovitz; Jerusalem: Wahrmann, 1966, p. 59), *b. Ḥul.* 24a (ברייתא), *Num. Rab.* 4:12.

[65] Yadin, *War Scroll*, 77–78. Cf. *m. 'Abot* 5:21 where לרדוף and לכח may also be taken as military terms.

This passage from the *Rule of the Congregation* again shows that the system of authority and communal structure envisaged for the end of days was a reflection of that practiced by the sect in their attempt to live the eschatological life in this world. Therefore, the age requirement of thirty for sectarian officials is evidence in the daily life of the sect of its dreams for the eschatological army, and its hopes for the future age. Here again we see the nexus of the desert heritage with the eschatological future. The very same communal and military organization which cemented the desert community of Israel was put into practice to the greatest extent possible by the sect, and would, in their view, be the new order for the eschatological community.

The Aged

The text now addresses the question of those not qualified to shoulder a normal share of the responsibilities of the life of the sect. Indeed, it is certain that this regulation, like the previous ones, reflected the custom of the sect in the present age as well as their dreams for the realization of the future. Our text mentions two kinds of disqualifications. The first is simply that of age. 1QSa 1:19–20 states:

וברובות שני איש, לפי כוחו ויתנ]ו משאו בנ]עבודן]ת העדה.

As the years of a man increase, according to his ability [they shall assign] him his duty in the [service] of the congregation.

Once the sectarian begins to grow old, his service to the eschatological community must be limited to that which he is still capable of performing. It appears from this passage that, if able, one might serve as an official of the community and take a full role in its affairs for as long as one lives. Yet other passages in the Qumran corpus would seem to indicate otherwise.

CD 10:4–10 specified that judges must not serve beyond the age of sixty because senility sets in at this age. After a description of the ten men who must be appointed as judges, the text specifies their ages:

. . . מבני חמשה ועשרים שנה עד בני ששים שנה. ואל יתיצב עוד מבן ששים שנה ומעלה לשפוט את העדה. כי במעל האדם מעטו ימו, ובחרון אף אל ביושבי הארץ אמר לסור את דעתם עד לא ישלימו את ימיהם.

. . . from twenty-five years old[66] to sixty years old. But let no one over sixty years old take his stand[67] to judge the congregation. For because of man's

---

[66] For the minimum age of twenty-five, see above p. 20. For a complete discussion of the ages of the judges at Qumran, see Schiffman, *Sectarian Law*, 30–37.

[67] For the forensic use of the התפעל of יצב, see Num 11:16 (Rabin, *Zadokite Documents*, 50). Note also Job 33:5 where it is used for answering a charge (BDB, 426).

transgression,[68] his days[69] diminished, and because of God's wrath[70] with the inhabitants of the earth, He decided to remove[71] their understanding before[72] they complete their days.

What exactly is meant by "God's wrath with the inhabitants of the earth?" It is tempting to suggest that it refers to Adam's fall, yet יושבי הארץ ("the inhabitants of the earth") could not properly be used to describe Adam and Eve but must mean humanity in general. Although "God's wrath" was indeed kindled against the generation of Noah (Gen. 6:5–8), the flood resulted, not senility. *Jub.* 3:11 and rabbinic parallels[73] suggest that it was in the time of Abraham that senility began to appear and man's life span was no longer as great as before. Yet there is no specific cause of "wrath" that can be pointed out as the reason for God's having introduced senility into the world.

Further, according to CD 14:6–7 the priest who mustered the assembly, probably to be identified with the פקיד ("overseer"), would end his service at sixty. In addition, CD 14:8–9 prohibits the מבקר ("examiner") from serving once he reached the age of fifty. Indeed, 1QM 7:1–2 provides that:

ואנשי הסרך יהיו מבן ארבעים שנה ועד בן חמישים; וסורכי המחנות יהיו
מבן חמישים שנה ועד ששים.

[68] Rabin translates our passage, "When man sinned . . . when God waxed wrath . . ." (*Zadokite Documents*, 50). He is taking the preposition ‑ב in a temporal sense whereas our translation reflects a causal relation, the *bet pretii* (GKC sec. 119p.).

[69] Phonetic spelling of the plural possessive (without י) is common at Qumran.

[70] Schechter's emendation to בחרות (cf. Ps 124:3) is ill-advised in light of the parallelism with מעל, a noun, not an infinitive (*Fragments*, XLVIII [80]). In the Bible, the phrase אף חרון occurs either with the Tetragrammaton or with a pronoun, only once with אלהים (Ezra 10:14) and never with אל. No doubt, our text is following the Qumran custom of avoiding the Tetragrammaton.

[71] M. H. Segal suggests that we read הפעיל, לסיר with elided ה ("ספר ברית דמשק," *Ha-Shiloah* 26 [1912] 499). His view is supported by what we now know about this linguistic phenomemon at Qumran (Licht, מגילת הסרכים, 46, cf. GKC sec. 53q) as well as by the similarity of the letters ו and י in the Dead Sea Scrolls (see Schiffman, *Halakhah at Qumran*, 30–31, n. 61). This is certainly the simplest interpretation. Nevertheless, if Rabin is correct in seeing this clause as a quotation from *Jub.* 23:11, his analysis as a קל and translation "He commanded that their understanding should depart . . ." would be better. Rabin notes that the Latin: *et erunt transeuntes ab ipsis spiritus intellectus eorum* (see R. H. Charles, *The Ethiopic Version of the Hebrew Book of Jubilees* [Oxford: Clarendon Press, 1895]) supports his view. He suggests that the peculiar Hebrew form of accusative with infinitive may lie behind this Latin text. Rabin rejects reading לסיר since then אמר "could only mean 'He intended'" (Rabin, *Zadokite Documents*, 51). I fail to see why this understanding of אמר would be objectionable.

[72] See Prov 8:26 (Segal, "ספר ברית דמשק," 499.). Rabin compares Targumic עד לא and Christian Palestinian Aramaic עדלא ד‑ as opposed to Syriac, Galilean, Babylonian עד דלא (*Zadokite Documents*, 51). His suggestion that the Hebrew has here conditioned the Aramaic usage is unlikely in light of the already established influence of Aramaic on Qumran Hebrew (Licht, מגילת הסרכים, 44–45).

[73] Cf. L. Ginzberg, *The Legends of the Jews* (Philadelphia: Jewish Publication Society, 1968) 5. 276, n. 36. On the notion that Abraham was the first to show signs of old age, see 5. 258, n. 272.

The men of the Serekh shall be from forty to fifty years old; the camp prefects shall be from fifty to sixty years old.

Here we see that the sectarian is expected to cease actual combat at the age of fifty, and then he may remain an administrative officer for another ten years. After sixty, he may no longer take part in the eschatological war of the sect.

Sixty is the highest age of all those mentioned in the scroll, and it is apparent that the role of סורכי המחנות ("camp prefects") was given to the oldest men still serving in the eschatological army. While it would be understandable that older men would not be efficient in a military context, their exclusion must also have been the result of the desire to insure perfection and purity in all the military operations of the sect.

How can we explain these maximum ages for administrative, judicial and military service? After all, Num 4:3, 23, 30, 35 and 47 fix the end of Levitical service at age fifty. Yadin correctly notes that according to Num 8:25–26, while active service for Levites ceased at fifty, certain subsidiary duties were continued after fifty. Such is the case in the *War Scroll* as well. Those reaching the age of fifty no longer went forth to active battle. They might continue to serve militarily in the subsidiary position of סורכי המחנות, camp prefects. Such service had to end at sixty. Others, it should be noted, from age fifty, served as part of the משמרות (or מעמדות, 1QM 2:4–5). The text of the *War Scroll* specifies no mandatory retirement from this function, although we might assume sixty in light of the parallels.[74]

1QSa 2:7–8 lists the feeble old man (איש זקן[ן] כושל) among those afflicted with impurities or physical defects who may not take their place among the congregation. It is clear from lines 9–10 that congregation (עדה) here refers to the assembly of the community. The text specifically states that the reason for exclusion of such people is that the holy angels are among the community. Those with disabilities would not be permitted to be in the presence of the angels.

Indeed, the very same explanation appears in 1QM 7:6 for the exclusion from going to war of women, young men, and those with various types of physical blemishes or impurities.[75] Nevertheless, this passage does not mention the feeble old man. Of course, it is known from other passages in the *War Scroll* that no one over sixty was allowed to have any role in the military service of the sect. Perhaps to some extent this desire to ensure maximum purity and perfection was operating in the exclusion of old men from the military, although the practical military considerations would be paramount.[76]

---

[74] Yadin, *War Scroll*, 78. 11QTemple 57:3 specifies sixty as the maximum age of military service.

[75] Cf. Yadin, *War Scroll*, 72–73.

[76] That man's military prowess decreases with age is stated in *Mekhilta' De-Rabbi Ishmael, Shirah* 4 (ed. Horovitz-Rabin, p. 130) and *Mekhilta' De-Rabbi Shim'on ben Yohai* to Exod 15:3 (ed. J. N. Epstein and E. Z. Melamed; Jerusalem: Mekize Nirdamim, 1955, p. 81; ed. D.

In an effort to explain the basis on which military service ceased at sixty, Yadin cites Lev 27:3, which he translates, "Then the valuation shall be for the male from twenty years old even unto sixty years old." Such a derivation would certainly violate the context of the Scriptural passage in question, but context was never a deterrent to the sect nor to the rabbinic interpreters of the Bible. Indeed, as Rabin notes, this passage prescribes sixty as the "limit of full value."[77]

Lev 27:3 would have served to indicate for the sect the upper limits of military service. They would have used it in a legal midrash to interpret Num 8:25 where it is indicated that subsidiary Levitical service might continue beyond fifty, but where no age limit was set. This exegesis would have allowed the sect to assume a limit of sixty years of age for this subsidiary service. Accordingly, the sect would allow no one, neither judge, soldier, nor official, to serve beyond sixty.

The sect, both in the present and the end of days, was rigorously stratified. Not only did this stratification extend to the abilities, piety, and purity of the sectarian, as we would gather from the other texts, but from our text we can see that it extended as well to the age of the individual. The sectarian would progress from the days of his early childhood education, to his religious majority, to the age of sectarian responsibility and finally, to the age of retirement.

This progression of ages has its parallel in the well-known *m. 'Abot* 5:21. The main contrast is clear, however. Whereas the tannaitic text envisages a life of Torah, in the Pharisaic-rabbinic sense, the sectarian document envisages a life of eschatological struggle. Hence, the *'Abot* text is centered on the acquisition of knowledge of the Torah and the practice of the commandments, the achievement of learning, and the honor due to the learned. On the other hand, the sectarian progresses from legal maturity to a series of roles in the military and eschatological preparations of the sect.

The Mentally Incompetent

The text of the *Rule of the Congregation* also deals with one who is unable to serve due to mental incompetence. 1QSa 1:20–22 discusses such people:

וכול איש פיתי אל יבוא בגורל להתיצב על עדת ישראל לרי[נ]ב ומן[שפט
ולשאת משא עדה ולהתיצב במלחמה להכניע גויים. [ר]ק[ן] בסרך [הצ]בא
יכתוב משפחתו. ובעבודת המס יעשה עבודתו כפי מעשו.

Hoffmann; Frankfurt a.M.: J. Kaufmann, 1905, p. 61). Cf. S. Kraus, פרס ורומי (Jerusalem: Mosad Harav Kook, 1948) 219.
[77] Rabin, *Zadokite Documents*, 50.

And any mentally incompetent[78] man shall not enter into full status to take his stand over the congregation of Israel, to stru[ggle for justice] and to bear the burden (of service) for the congregation, and to take his stand in battle to subdue (the) nations. [Rather,] he (the examiner?) shall inscribe his (the incompetent's) family in the roster of [the ar]my. And regarding corvée labor, he shall perform his service according to his ability.

The use of the root פתי in Scripture would lead to the suggestion that the פתי suffers only from insufficient mental ability to undertake the normal civic, religious and military duties of the sect and to discharge them appropriately. On the other hand, the parallels between the use of פתי in the sectarian literature and the use of שוטה in rabbinic texts would suggest otherwise. The שוטה is a madman, or one who is insane. In any case, the פתי is to be excluded from leadership in the sect, as well as from serving in a military context. Indeed, CD 13:4–7 provides that if the priest is a פתי, he shall be guided by the מבקר ("examiner") in matters of quarantine:

ואם משפט לתורת נגע יהיה באיש, ובא הכהן ועמד במחנה והבינו המבקר
בפרוש התורה. ואם פתי הוא, הוא יסגירנו כי להם המשפט.

And if there be a case of [the law of] "(If there be a plague on a man,"[79] then the priest shall come and stand in the camp and the examiner shall instruct him in the specification(s) of the Torah. For (even) if he (the priest) be a פתי, he shall quarantine him, for judgment is theirs (the priests).[80]

The *War Scroll* makes no explicit mention of exclusion of the פתי from military service. It may be that his exemption is implied by the description of the soldiers found in the law of conscription of 1QM 7:5:

כולם יהיו אנשי נדבת מלחמה ותמימי רוח ובשר.

All of them shall be volunteers for battle and perfect in spirit and body.

On the other hand, there are detailed lists of those excluded from military service in the *War Scroll*. The absence of the פתי from these lists might imply that he might serve. That military considerations alone would exclude him is obvious. That the sect would desire to preclude him from positions of sectarian responsibility in the present, the eschatological battle, and the end of days would also result not only from practical considerations but also from the sect's view that such individuals would detract from the perfect holiness it sought to achieve.

[78] Cf. CD 13:4–7 and our note on פתי in Schiffman, *Halakhah at Qumran*, 39–40, n. 111.

[79] A reference to either Lev 13:9 or 29. The term תורה is used in the conclusion of this same chapter of Lev (v. 29).

[80] For additional commentary, see Schiffman, *Halakhah at Qumran*, 39–40.

2
THE COUNCIL OF THE COMMUNITY

The Levites

The *Rule of the Congregation* now turns to the functions of the Levites. 1QSa 1:23–25 describes their role in the sect:

וכני לוי יעמדו איש במעמדו, על פי בני אהרון, להביא ולהוציא את כול
העדה, איש כסרכו, על ידי ראשי [אבות] העדה, לשרים ולשופטים ולשוטרים
למספר כול צבאותם, על פי בני צדוק הכוהנים [וכול ר]אשי אבות העדה.

And the Levites shall take their stand, each in his position, according to the sons of Aaron, to bring in and to lead out the entire congregation,[1] each according to his (place in the) roster, at the hand of the heads of [the households] of the Congregation, as officers, as judges, and as provosts, according to the number of all their hosts, according to the Sons of Zadok the priests, [and all the he]ads of the clans of the congregation.

Here the role of the Levites is not that of cultic officials. Indeed, we would expect that in the sect's view, as in that of the prophet Ezekiel, the non-Zadokite priests would have fulfilled the role of temple assistants.[2] Instead, the Levites appear here, as also in Chronicles,[3] as officers of various kinds. They are to have specific duties, called מעמד ("position"), and they are to serve in maintaining the sectarian roster (סרך)[4] and in mustering the members of the eschatological community. In this regard, as in every other aspect of sectarian life, they do so at the instruction of the Zadokite priests and the heads of the clans of the congregation.

The specific functions of the Levites are termed מעמד ("position"). This term had various connotations for the sect. Rabbinic מעמד referred to a group of Israelites who assembled to recite biblical passages while the priestly representatives of their town officiated in the Jerusalem temple. This

---

[1] Num 27:17, referring to Joshua.
[2] See L. H. Schiffman, *Halakhah at Qumran* (Leiden: E. J. Brill, 1975) 72–75.
[3] 1 Chr 23:4; 2 Chr 34:13; cf. 1 Chr 15:16; 2 Chr 35:9; and 1QM 7:13 (J. Licht, מגילת הסרכים [Jerusalem: Mosad Bialik, 1965] 260). Cf. D. Schwartz, "סופרים ופרושים חנפים—מי הם 'הסופרים' בברית החדשה?", *Zion* 50 (1984/85) 123–29.
[4] See Schiffman, *Halakhah at Qumran*, 65–67 on the sectarian rosters.

usage is not found at Qumran, despite the fact that the very same institution is envisaged in 1QM 2:4–5.

Yadin has discussed the use of this term in Qumran literature. He notes that the author of the *War Scroll* used מעמד "to describe the position of the soldiers when they stand arrayed for combat."[5] He also observes that this term is used in regard to the annual mustering and covenant renewal for the "body containing the priests, levites, and Israelites (each group according to its own subdivision)."[6] The בית מעמד of 1QS 2:19–24 is the correct position of each member of the sect in the formation.[7] In using this term to describe the role of the Levites in the eschatological community, the author of the *Rule of the Congregation* has drawn on the common military and cultic terminology of the sect, all of which in fact was derived from the pattern of Israelite wilderness life depicted in the Bible. Here too, the historical, the cultic, the military, and the eschatological were all intertwined in the language of the sect.

Although it is possible to read our text as mandating that the officials mentioned here, officers, judges and provosts, must all be Levites, this interpretation is most unlikely. Levitical judges and provosts are known among the officials of the sect, but a claim of exclusivity on their behalf is nowhere made. It seems, rather, that in our text the Levites are to "bring in and out" the congregation of the end of days, that is to supervise the mustering, so that each member of the community is in his proper place, according to the appropriate officials who are to oversee his actions. The preposition ל before the designations of the various officials would indicate, then, that it is under the supervision of these officials that the members of the sect are to present themselves at the eschatological mustering. It is to that assembly that the *Rule of the Congregation* now turns.

The Functions and Purity of the Assembly

1QSa 1:25–27 is an introduction specifying the functions of the assembly and the requirement that all who attend be ritually pure:

ואם תעודה תהיה לכול הקהל למשפט או לעצת יחד או לתעודת מלחמה,
וקדשום שלושת ימים להיות כול הבא עתוד לעצ[ה].

And if there shall be a convocation of all the congregation[8] for judgment

---

[5] Y. Yadin, *The Scroll of the War of the Sons of Light against the Sons of Darkness* (Oxford: Oxford University Press, 1962) 146.

[6] Ibid., 206–7.

[7] Licht, מגילת הסרכים, 72–73.

[8] Barthélemy notes that the expression כל הקהל ("the whole assembly") is typical of the Chronicler, to whom he also ascribes Ezra and Nehemiah (D. Barthélemy and J. T. Milik, *Qumran Cave I*, Discoveries in the Judaean Desert 1 [Oxford: Clarendon Press, 1955] 116).

or for a council of the community, or for a convocation of war, they shall sanctify them(selves)[9] for three days, so that everyone who comes shall be pre[pared for the coun]cil.[10]

The occasion for the meeting of the assembly described in our text is referred to with the word תעודה. While this term is usually taken to be derived from the root עוד, a denominative from the noun עד, "witness," examination of the uses of this word in Qumran literature will show that the sect took it as derived from the root יעד. The sect therefore understood תעודה as that which is appointed to happen by divine decree. In the expression מועדי תעודתם, "their appointed times," this term refers to the stages in the history of the sect's interpretations of the law.[11] In our passage, the word תעודה must therefore denote an occasion at which one of the matters taken up below in the text must be considered. For want of a better term, we will use "convocation," since it conveys the aspect of joining together, a common usage of the root יעד.[12] The three functions of the convocations are described as משפט, עצת היחד, and תעודת מלחמה. We shall examine each in turn.

The term משפט ("judgment") is variously used in legal contexts in the Bible. Our examination of the legal usage of this term in the Dead Sea Scrolls

---

Indeed, in these books, this expression refers to the entire Jewish community, usually when it takes some official political or religious action.

[9] The explanations of Barthélemy and Licht would require the more literal translation, "they (the Levites) shall sanctify them." This interpretation is based upon the fact that the Levites are the subject of the previous sentence in 1QSa 1:22–25. This seems unlikely, however, since there is no indication in Exod 19:14–15, which served as the basis of this passage, that the purification rituals were to be performed by the Levites. In fact, as we will explain below, the specific requirements of this purificatory process can be gleaned from this parallel. It may be that the root קדש should be translated here "purify." Cf. 1QS 3:4 and the references in Licht, מגילת הסרכים, 78.

[10] Barthélemy restores here עת]יד ל[הנה, with a question mark over the first ה. He translates, "afin que tous les participants soient prêts *pour la date fixée*" (italics are his). He compares Esth 3:14 and 8:13 (DJD 1. 115–16). Despite his comments, the translation is difficult to understand in light of his restoration. He is followed in his restoration by H. N. Richardson, "Some Notes on 1QSa," *JBL* 76 (1957) 114. Richardson, however, suggests understanding להנה as the first word of the next sentence. He therefore translates, "rea[dy. For such] purposes. . . ." Barthélemy read the first letter after the lacuna as a ה since he judged the right part of the preserved part of the letter too low for a צ. Licht notes that this reading is also not without its difficulty, as it would require that the end of the "roof" of the ה be written very low (מגילת הסרכים, 263). For this reason, we follow Licht and J. Carmignac, "La Règle de la congrégation," *Les Textes de Qumran* (ed. J. Carmignac, É. Cothenet and H. Lignée; Paris: Letouzey and Ané, 1963) 2. 22 in reading לעצ[ה. Licht's reading עתוד follows the כתיב of Esth 8:13 while Barthélemy's עתיד follows the קרי of Esth 8:13 and the text of 3:14.

[11] See Schiffman, *Halakhah at Qumran*, 27, n. 41.

[12] This is the translation of Barthélemy and Carmignac (French "convocation") and Richardson. Licht's explanation, תפקיד שנועד לקהל, does not take sufficient account of the use of this root in Qumran passages, despite the references he gives (מגילת הסרכים, 263).

shows that in most cases, it refers to the sectarian regulations. These, in turn, are derived by the sect through inspired biblical exegesis.[13] On the other hand, the meaning in this passage must be taken as that of judgment, that is, the rendering of legal decisions in specific cases. The same usage occurs in 1QS 6:8–13 in the description of the מושב הרבים, the sectarian legislative and judicial assembly.[14] In fact, one of the main functions of the מושב הרבים was to serve as the highest court in the daily life of the Qumran sect. In the messianic vision of the sect, the council which our text from the *Rule of the Congregation* describes was to assume the very same function as that of the מושב הרבים.

The second function of the assembly is what is termed עצת היחד ("council of the community"). This phrase, in this context, cannot simply refer to all matters to be decided by the assembly. Clearly, it is limited here to those matters not of forensic or military nature. This would then refer to the acts of sectarian exegesis and the codification of the law as decided by the sect. It designates the decisions pertaining to the sect's organization and structure as well. Finally, it must also involve decisions about the status of members. Granted, in the end of days all Israel, in the dreams of the sect, would enter into the community; there would not be an issue of membership. Yet within the sect, status would still have to be determined, and this function would be accomplished by the assembly.

The final purpose of this assembly is to declare war. The term תעודת מלחמה ("convocation of war") must refer to the convocation at which war is to be declared.[15] This aspect is most significant, for it allows us to determine at what stage in the unfolding *eschaton* the assembly we have discussed is to come into existence. The *War Scroll* pictures a series of battles and a cycle of victories that will lead to the final end of days. Thereafter, when all the enemies of Israel have been destroyed, and all Israel has either repented and become part of the sect or has been extirpated, then there will be eternal peace. Our text, which concerns the decision as to whether or not to go to war, must refer to an assembly that would come into existence at the very onset of the *eschaton*. Indeed, after some sign that the end of days had dawned, it was this assembly that would make the decision to set into effect the series of events described in the *War Scroll*. This body would preside over the sect's role in these final battles.[16]

---

[13] Schiffman, *Halakhah at Qumran*, 42–47.

[14] Ibid., 68–70.

[15] Note the expression תעודות המלחמה in 1QM 2:8 (Licht, מגילת הסרכים, 263) which Yadin's edition translates, "the pre-ordained periods of war," and ותעודות ישועה לעם פדותו, "times ordained for salvation for the people to be redeemed by Him" in 1QM 14:4. Yadin calls attention to תעודות שלום in 1Q 36 frag. 1 (DJD 1. 138). Cf. Yadin, *War Scroll*, 80–81.

[16] On the relationship of the *Rule of the Congregation* and the *War Scroll*, see Licht, מגילת הסרכים, 248–49.

These three functions can be compared with those of the later tannaitic בית דין הגדול ("great court") also termed the Sanhedrin. This court of seventy-one was to be the final recourse for decisions on all criminal matters, both those which had originated in lower courts and those capital matters which originated in this body. Like the assembly of the sect in the end of days, the rabbinic Sanhedrin would be the final arbiter of matters of law. Finally, declaration of war could only be made upon the decision of the Great Sanhedrin. Only this authority could decide if a war was justified and permitted according to the law of the Torah as understood by the tannaim.[17]

The sect required a special state of purity for attendance at a session of the eschatological assembly. Our text tells us that a three day purification ritual was necessary. No doubt this rite was based on the three days of preparation which the children of Israel observed before the revelation at Sinai (Exod 19:10–11, 14–15). According to the biblical account, the Israelites abstained from sexual relations, washed their garments, and, if the use of קדש ("to sanctify") may be taken as an indication, performed some form of ablutions.[18] To the sect, joining in this convocation required the very same level of sanctity and purification, for the actions of this body were seen by the sect as a continuation of the revelation at Sinai. Indeed, the concept of inspired biblical exegesis as the basis of Qumran law assumes that the members of the sect were acting under divine inspiration at the sessions of the assembly. Further on, the scroll will provide additional details regarding the purity of the eschatological assembly and these will be discussed below.

The Participants

The *Rule of the Congregation* continues with a list of those who are to attend the assembly (1QSa 1:27–2:3):

אלה האנשים הנקראים לעצת היחד: כול חנכמי העדה והנבונים והידעים, תמימי הדרך ואנושי החיל, עם]שרי השב[טים וכול שופטיהם ושוטריהם ושרי האלפים ושרי]ם למאות[ולחמשים ולעשרות, והלויים בתו]ך מחלקת עבו[ד]תו. אלה אנושי השם קוראי מועד הנועדים לעצת היחד בישראל לפני בני צדוק הכוהנים.

These are the men[19] who have been invited to the council of the

---

[17] Cf. L. H. Schiffman, "Legislation concerning Relations with Non-Jews in the *Zadokite Fragments* and Rabbinic Literature," *RQ* 11 (1983) 379–89.

[18] Barthélemy (DJD 1. 116) and Licht (מגילת הסרכים, 263) also compare Ezra 10:8–9 which, however, has no relation to a purification ritual. For the meaning of קדש, see Ibn Ezra to Exod 19:10. That the sect would have understood the root קדש in this manner can be seen from 1QS 3:4 and the material cited in Licht, מגילת הסרכים, 78.

[19] On the strange writing of האנשים in the MS, cf. Licht, ibid. While the MS is unclear, the correct reading is certain.

community:[20] All the sa[ges of the] congregation and the scholars and the knowledgeable ones, of perfect path and men of valor, with the [officers of the tri]bes[21] and all their judges and their provosts and the officers of thousands, and the officer[s[22] for hundreds], and for fifties, and for tens, and the Levites, a[mong the divi]sion of his service.[23] These are the men of renown, invited for the occasion,[24] who assemble for the co[uncil of the communi]ty in Israel, before the Sons of Zadok, the priests.

Several aspects of this text require extensive comment. First, like the somewhat shorter description of those who will attend the messianic meal found in 1QSa 2:14–17,[25] this text is based on Deut 1:9–18. In this passage Moses describes to the children of Israel how he set up the judicial and administrative system of the nation for the period of desert wandering. A narrative parallel to this passage is found in Exod 18:13–26.[26] The presence of the phrase אנושי החיל ("men of valor") in our passage shows that it has been directly influenced by the Exodus material, although its structure is primarily derived from the Deuteronomy passage. It would appear that תמימי הדרך ("ones of perfect path") in our passage serves as an exegesis which clarifies the character of the officials in Exod 18:21. The sect has substituted an epithet of itself for the Bible's "who fear God, trustworthy men who spurn ill-gotten gain."[27] To the Qumranites, membership in the sect is a *sine qua non*

[20] The scribe wrote מבן עש and then realized his error. He therefore left a space to indicate erasure. His error was probably caused by confusion with 1QSa 1:8 ובן עשרים which he had just written. Cf. 1QSa 1:12 for the same phenomenon (Licht, מגילת הסרכים, 263).

[21] Vermes restores ראשי, but cf. 1 Chr 27:22, 28:1 and 29:6 (Barthélemy, DJD 1. 116). Richardson, "Some Notes," 114 and n. 42, restores ויודעי לוקטים, which he translates, "[those who know sec]rets." This is highly unlikely, however.

[22] The omission of the final מ after the lacuna in Barthélemy's restoration (DJD 1. 110) seems to be a typographical error.

[23] Restoring with Barthélemy, Licht, Carmignac and Richardson. The words לוים, מחלקות, and עבודה appear together in 1 Chr 28:13, 21; 2 Chr 31:2; and 35:10. Cf. 1 Chr 23:6; 2 Chr 8:14; and 23:8. 1 Chr 27:1 mentions the officiers of thousands and hundreds and their bailiffs along with המחלקות.

[24] Based on Num 16:2. The phrase recurs below in 1QSa 2:11 and 13. Cf. also 1QS 2:6–7 and 3:3–4 (Carmignac, *Textes*, 2. 23). Barthélemy reads קיראי (DJD, 1. 110) while Licht (מגילת הסרכים, 263) reads קוראי. It is virtually impossible to distinguish ו from י in most MSS from Qumran. The reading קוראי would be explained as a shift from פעול to פועל, a phenomenon known in the Qumran texts (cf. Barthélemy, DJD 1. 116 and Licht, מגילת הסרכים, 264). Note the interchange of קרואי and קריאי in the Masoretic notes to the Pentateuch (Num 1:16, 26:9). For the translation "invited," cf. Rashi to Num 1:16.

[25] See Chapter Four on the messianic communal meal.

[26] The major difference between the passages is that the Exodus narrative portrays Jethro as the stimulus for the entire reorganization of the administrative and judicial system, whereas he is absent from the Deuteronomic account. Deuteronomy makes Moses the originator of the reform.

[27] So new JPS. The phrase תמימי דרך occurs in Ps 119:1 and Prov 11:20. As Carmignac notes, the phrase occurs in 1QS 4:22; 1QM 14:7; 1QH 1:36 and 4Q *Serekh Shirot ʿOlat Ha-Shabbat* A,

for leadership in the eschatological community.

According to Deuteronomy, the sages and wise men are to serve as the officials. It is they whom Moses appoints to the various positions of authority. Indeed, the same impression is gained from comparison with Exod 18:21 and 25. The sect, however, interpreted Deuteronomy to mean that distinct leaders and sages were appointed. The sages and wise men would serve as judges and teachers. Besides them there was to be an entire series of officers connected with military conscription. These two groups, in the view of the sect, led the people in the desert period. The very same two classes of officialdom would guide the sect in the end of days. If there is any question about this interpretation of the sectarian passage, one has only to compare the description of the messianic banquet, which appears further on in 1QSa 2:11–17 (discussed below in Chapter Four), in which the sages and the officials of the sect are clearly to be distinguished.

Let us now look at the specific classes to be involved in this assembly. The sages and wise men are described as תמימי הדרך ("ones of perfect path"). This term is used in the Dead Sea Scrolls to refer to the sect. In fact, the word תמים ("perfect") in all its forms is regularly applied to the sect and to the life of perfection that membership in it is intended to engender. Clearly, the sages of the future age are to be those who are members of the sect in the present age. But can we say anything else about these sages? The *Manual of Discipline* speaks at length about the משכיל (1QS 9:12–26). The משכיל, literally "enlightened one," is apparently one of the sect's terms for its sages and models of piety. These individuals were recognized for their intellectual and moral greatness, while not necessarily being assigned any specific function.[28] It may be that the sect expected these people to assume a more formal role in the end of days.

The officers over tribes, as well as judges and bailiffs and captains of thousands, hundreds, fifties and tens, are also to participate in the eschatological convocation. Indeed, the organization of the sect described here closely parallels that of the *War Scroll*. Yadin, in discussing the relevant passages in the *War Scroll*, has observed that in this regard the pattern of sectarian organization for the eschatological battle was the same as that followed in the present life of the sect. CD 12:22–13:2 shows that annual mustering must have been part of the ritual calendar of the sect, as can be gathered as well from 1QS 2:19–22.[29] From 1QSa 1:13–15 we learn that these officers had to be at least thirty years of age.[30]

---

line 22 (*Textes*, 2. 23). Cf. L. H. Schiffman, "*Merkavah* Speculation at Qumran: The 4Q *Serekh Shirot 'Olat ha-Shabbat*," *Mystics, Philosophers, and Politicians, Essays in Jewish Intellectual History in Honor of Alexander Altmann* (ed. J. Reinharz, D. Swetschinski, with K. P. Bland; Durham: Duke University Press, 1982) 30.

[28] On משכיל, cf. Schiffman, *Halakhah at Qumran*, 25, n. 24 and the sources cited there.

[29] Yadin, *War Scroll*, 59–61.

[30] See Schiffman, *Sectarian Law*, 34–35 and above, pp. 21–23.

Interestingly, the Levites are mentioned here as "among the division of his service." The term מחלקת ("division," "course") for the divisions of the priests and Levites figures prominently in the book of Chronicles.[31] The Levites are not listed among those who are to attend the messianic communal meal in 1QSa 2:11–22, although it can be assumed that the שוטרים ("bailiffs") were Levites, in light of tannaitic and Josephan parallels.[32] Indeed, the Levites are frequently designated in the *War Scroll*, and again we have a parallel between the organizational patterns of the two texts.

Finally, this passage specifies that this עצת היחד ("council of the community") is going to take place "before the sons of Zadok, the priests." The leadership of the Zadokite priesthood in the sect has been discussed extensively. According to numerous sectarian texts they are the original leaders who organized the sect and who constituted the main authority figures in the early days of the sect.[33] It seems, however, that at some point their role became ceremonial, so that they officially presided over the מושב הרבים (the sectarian assembly) without actually having full power as the sect became more democratized.[34] The sect expected that the Zadokite priests would preside over the assembly of the end of days.[35] The long list of other officials who would participate in the eschatological convocation leads to the conclusion that the Zadokites were expected to have a minimum of real authority in the new assembly.

The Future as a Mirror of the Present

The *Rule of the Congregation* serves another function due to the close parallelism between the communal meals of the sect in the present premessianic age and those expected to occur in the end of days. Indeed, the sect ate its communal meals in the present in expectation of those of the future age. For this reason, they ate under conditions of perfect ritual purity. Because of the manner in which the sect attempted to realize the *eschaton* already in its own present-day life, certain details about the eschatological meal can be assumed to have been characteristic as well of the meal in the present pre-messianic age.[36] Therefore, it is possible to use the *Rule of the Congregation* as a guide to practice in the present age due to this mirroring of the future.

---

[31] E.g., 1 Chr 23:6; 24:1; 26:1, 12, 19; 2 Chr 8:14; 31:2; 35:4, 10.

[32] Josephus, *Ant.* 4.8.14 §214; *Sifre Devarim* 144 (ed. L. Finkelstein; New York: Jewish Theological Seminary, 1969, p. 197). Cf. Schiffman, *Sectarian Law*, 42, n. 17 and Yadin, *War Scroll*, 152.

[33] Cf. Schiffman, *Halakhah at Qumran*, 70–75.

[34] Cf. Schiffman, *Sectarian Law*, 5.

[35] Cf. 1QSa 1:2 and 24 in which the Zadokite priests figure prominently.

[36] Cf. Chapter Four on the messianic banquet.

Evidence points in the same direction regarding the comparison between the מושב הרבים (the sectarian assembly) of the present pre-messianic age described in the *Manual of Discipline* and the convocation of our eschatologically oriented text, the *Rule of the Congregation*. Indeed, the three categories of subject matter for the agenda of convocations in 1QSa 1:25–26 are almost identical to those of the parallel in 1QS 6:9–10, except that the eschatological text adds the council of war, a matter which was simply of no consequence in the pre-messianic period described by the *Manual*. The parallels between the terminology of the two passages are even more extensive, among the more interesting being that of 1QS 6:11–13 and 1QSa 2:9–11.

It can therefore be suggested, based on the material presented here, that the sectarian assembly is constituted and functions in similar manner in both the pre-messianic and messianic ages. At the very least, the regulations detailed in 1QS 6:8–13, would apply to the messianic assembly as well. One can assume that the same prohibitions on interrupting would be in force. The same order of speakers, according to status in the sect, would be observed. Those wishing to speak would need the permission of the presiding official.

A more difficult question is whether the reverse is also true. Can we extrapolate from the rules for the messianic assembly to those of the present age? We would maintain that we can, in view of the other parallels which can be demonstrated. We would then expect that the officers of thousands, hundreds, fifties and tens, as well as the judges and their bailiffs, would all have participated in the מושב הרבים (the sectarian assembly).

Can we also say that the laws of purity maintain this same reciprocal relationship? The messianic assembly requires a special purification period before its meeting. While such a period is nowhere described in the texts referring to the present age, we may assume that the very same rituals would have been observed. After all, the deliberations and decisions of the מושב הרבים (the sectarian assembly) were, for the sect, a continuation of the revelation at Sinai. In Chapter Three we will examine the rules regarding those excluded from the eschatological convocation because of physical deformity, disease or old age. It is most probable that the very same classes of people excluded in the end of days were excluded from the sectarian assembly in the present age as well.

---

[37] We cannot know if, in the end of days, the מבקר ("examiner") was to be replaced by the messiah as the presiding officer of the assembly (cf. Licht, מגילת הסרכים, 266). Indeed, the messianic figures are explicitly mentioned in regard to the eschatological meal in 1QSa 2:11–17, but do not appear in our text in regard to the assembly.

3

THE ASSEMBLY AT
THE END OF DAYS

Exclusion from the Council of the Community

The *Rule of the Congregation* presents a detailed list of those who are to be excluded from the council of the community because of impurity, physical impairment, or advanced age (1QSa 2:3–11):

וכול איש מנוגע [באחת מכ]ול טומאות האדם אל יבוא בקהל אלה. וכול איש
מנוגע בן אלה לבלתין החזיק מעמד בתוך העדה: וכול מנוגע בבשרו, נכאן ה
רגלים או ידים, [פסח]ח או [עור], או חרש או אלם, או מום מנוגע [בבשרן
לראות עינים; או איש זקון כושל לבלתן[י התחזק בתוך העדה; אל יבן ואן
אלה להתיצב [בתוך] עדת [אנו]שן שי השם כיא מלאכי קודש [בעצ]תם. ואם יש
[ד]בר לאחד מא]לה לדבר אל עצת הקודש וח]דורשן יהון מפיהו ואל תוך [העדה
לו אן יבוא האיש כיא מנוגע ה[וא.

And any man who is afflicted[1] [with any one of][2] the human uncleannesses[3] shall not enter into the congregation[4] of these.[5] And anyone who is afflicted

---

[1] Translating in light of Ps 73:5 which is the only case of the פועל of נגע in the Bible. Note that אדם occurs in that verse. On the other hand, the use of this root in the קל in Lev 5:3, which has clearly influenced our passage, might require a translation, "who has come in contact with. . . ." Licht notes that this verb in tannaitic usage refers only to houses and garments (cf. *m. Neg.* 13:6–7, etc.) but not to people (מגילת הסרכים [Jerusalem: Mosad Bialik, 1965] 264).

[2] Restored with the traces (Licht, מגילת הסרכים, 264, and H. N. Richardson, "Some Notes on 1QSa," *JBL* 76 [1957] 115).

[3] Translating with new JPS to Lev 5:3 on which see below, pp. 38–39.

[4] Cf. Deut 23:2–9; Lam 1:10; and Neh 13:1. While prevalent exegesis has taken this usage as referring to the prohibition on marriage, Lam 1:10 and our text seem to take this as referring to a prohibition on entry into the Israelite *sancta*, represented by the temple in Lamentations and the sectarian eschatological assembly in our passage.

[5] Barthélemy (D. Barthélemy and J. T. Milik, *Qumran Cave I*, Discoveries in the Judaean Desert 2 [Oxford: Clarendon Press, 1955] 117 and Carmignac ("La Règle de la Congrégation," *Le textes de Qumran* [ed. J. Carmignac, É. Cothenet and H. Lignée; Paris: Letouzey et Ané, 1963] 2. 23) emended to אל (cf. Deut 23:2–4) but Licht, (מגילת הסרכים, 264) regards this as unnecessary in light of the sect's tendency to avoid the use of the divine name. Y. Yadin, (*The Temple Scroll* [Jerusalem: Israel Exploration Society, 1983] 1. 291) understands אלה as the divine name אלוה. Cf. also J. Maier, *Die Texte vom Toten Meer* (Munich and Basel: Ernst Reinhardt, 1960) 2. 157.

with [these so as not to][6] take (his) stand[7] among the congregation:[8] And any who is afflicted in his flesh,[9] crippl[ed in the legs][10] or the hands, [lam]e or [blin]d[11] or deaf or dumb, or if he is stricken[12] with a blemish [in his flesh] visible to the eyes; or a tottering o[ld] man who [can]not maintain himself[13] among the congregation; these may not en[ter] to take (their) stand [among][14] the congregation of the [me]n of renown for holy angels [are in their coun]cil. But if one of these has [a matter][15] to say to the council of holiness,[16] [then] he shall examine [him] directly (lit. "from his mouth") but among [the congregation] the man [shall not] enter for h[e is af]flicted.[17]

Our passage is made up of several parts: 1QSa 2:3–4 contains a blanket prohibition to the effect that anyone who is impure may not enter into the council of the community. 2:4–7 prohibits those afflicted with various physical deformities or diseases from participation in the council. 2:7 prohibits the aged from taking part. 2:8–9 indicates that the reason for these prohibitions from participation in the council of the community in the end of days is the presence of the holy angels in the council. Finally, 2:9–11 provides that an official take a deposition in the event that such a person desires to present a matter to the council. Each one of these regulations will be considered in detail.

The Impure

1QSa 2:3–4 prohibits anyone who is stricken with any of the human uncleannesses from entering the council of the community in the end of days. The key to this prescription is the interpretation of the words טומאות האדם. J. Licht correctly notes that the text is referring here to a form of ritual impurity, rather than to some kind of a blemish or deformity. He maintains that this phrase refers to all forms of impurity. The phrase is derived from טומאת אדם ("human uncleanness") which occurs in Lev 5:3 and 7:21. Our author adapted the phrase and used it in the plural. The context in Lev 5:3 indicates that it refers to impurity of the dead as well as to those impurities

---

[6] Restoring with the unclear traces (Licht, מגילת הסרכים, 264).

[7] Cf. line 7, 1QH 4:36 and 5:29 (Licht, ibid.).

[8] Licht (ibid.) suggests that this sentence is a remnant of another version of the following statement which was copied in error. He suggests alternately that this may be a general statement preceding the details which follow. The second interpretation is followed here.

[9] Cf. Lev 13:2 for בשרו and נגע.

[10] Restored with unclear traces (Licht, ibid.).

[11] Licht notes that the letters פס and עו are not written clearly (ibid.).

[12] All these deformities are treated in detail below.

[13] Restored with traces (Licht, מגילת הסרכים, 265).

[14] Cf. above, n. 7.

[15] Restored with traces (Licht, ibid.)

[16] Cf. 1QS 6:12; CD 14:11.

[17] Carmignac (Texte, 2. 24) takes the next line of 1QSa as the continuation of this sentence.

which are imparted to a person by the various bodily fluxes. It is no doubt the intention of the author of the *Rule of the Congregation* to include these varieties of impurity, hence the use of the plural. Therefore, we may safely conclude that our text includes all forms of ritual impurity which a person may contract.[18]

This entire prescription can be compared with a passage in the *War Scroll* (1QM 7:3–6). Indeed, as noted by Yadin,[19] the regulations which were in effect for the eschatological council of the community were similar to those for the eschatological battle. 1QM 7:4–5 provides that:

‏. . . או איש מנוגע בטמאת בשרו, כול אלה לא ילכו אתם למלחמה.

... or a man who is afflicted with an uncleanness of his flesh, all these shall not go with them to battle.

This sentence is similar in wording to our text except that ‏טמאת בשרו, "an uncleanness of his flesh," appears where the *Rule of the Congregation* uses ‏טומאות האדם ("human uncleannesses"). 1QM 7:5–6 juxtaposes these impurities to another type, that of one who had a seminal emission:

‏וכול איש אשר לוא יהיה טהור ממקורו ביום המלחמה לא ירד אתם. . . .

And any man who is not pure in regard to his sexual organs[20] on the day of battle shall not join them in battle. . . .[21]

Yadin has noted the dependence of this regulation on Deut 23:11–12. According to him, those who have experienced seminal emissions are not excluded completely from the battlefield, yet they cannot take part in battle until they have been purified.[22] Yadin notes that this formulation is less severe than that regarding women and children who are excluded from the camp. He therefore suggests that those impure as a result of seminal emissions "may have served away from the actual battlefield."[23] While Yadin is certainly correct in noting that the formulation appears less severe, the source in Deuteronomy would indicate that those who had experienced seminal emissions were to

---

[18] Cf. *Sifra' Wa-Yiqra', Pereq* 12:8 (ed. I. H. Weiss; Vienna: J. Schlossberg, 1861–62, pp. 23b–c), *Midrash Ha-Gadol* to Lev 7:21 (ed. S. Fisch; Jerusalem: Mosad Harav Kook, 1972), M. Kasher, ‏תורה שלמה (Jerusalem: American Biblical Encyclopedia Society, 1975) 27. 77, n. 147. On the exclusion of the impure from priestly service, see Philo *Special Laws* 1. 118.

[19] Yadin, *Temple Scroll*, 1. 290–91.

[20] See the detailed note of Yadin (*The Scroll of the War of the Sons of Light against the Sons of Darkness* [Oxford: Oxford University Press, 1962] 291) as well as J. Carmignac, *La Règle de la Guerre* (Paris: Letouzey et Ané, 1958) 1. 106, and B. Jongeling, *Le Rouleau de la Guerre* (Assen: Van Gorcum, 1962) 196–97.

[21] Trans. in Yadin, *War Scroll*, 291. Cf. the reading in 4Q491 (M^a) which adds ‏[בלי]ן[לה ההואה, indicating that the impurity lasted only until the morning (M. Baillet, *Qumrân Grotte 4*, Discoveries in the Judaean Desert 7 [Oxford: Clarendon Press, 1982] 13).

[22] Yadin, *War Scroll*, 73. Cf. B. M. Bokser, "Approaching Sacred Space," *HTR* 78 (1985) 279–87.

[23] Yadin, *War Scroll*, 290.

be excluded from the camp until they had completed their required ablutions.

Yadin suggests that the expression טמאת בשרו ("uncleanness of his flesh") is meant to include all the forms of disease listed in Leviticus 13. Indeed, this verse does contain the word בשרו ("of his flesh") and may be the basis of the non-Pentateuchal term טמאת בשרו ("uncleanness of his flesh"). According to v. 46, such temporary diseases result in exclusion from the desert camp of Israel. On the other hand, it is possible that this phrase in the *War Scroll* refers to all impurities other than that resulting from seminal emission. Nevertheless, most probably טומאות האדם in *Rule of the Congregation* refers to all impurities, including that resulting from a seminal emission. If so, the laws for battle (not conscription) are in this case the same as those of the council of the community.

A parallel to this prescription is found in 11QTemple 45:7–12:

ואיש] כי יהיה לו מקרה לילה לוא יבוא אל כול המקדש עד אשר [ישנ]לים
שלושת ימים. וכבס בגדיו ורחץ ביום הראישון, וביום השלישי יכבס בגדיו
ורחץ. ובאה השמש, אחר יבוא אל המקדש. ולוא יבואו בנדת טמאתמה אל
מקדשי וטמאו. ואיש כיא ישכב עם אשתו שכבת זרע לוא יבוא אל כל עיר
המקדש אשר אשכין שמי בה שלושת ימים.

And if a m[an] has a nocturnal emission he may not enter the entire sanctuary until he [com]pletes three days. And he shall launder his clothes and wash on the first day, and on the third day he shall launder his clothes and wash. Then after the sun has set, he may enter the sanctuary. They may not enter my sanctuary in their time of impurity so as to render it impure. And when a man has sexual relations with his wife he may not enter the entire city of the sanctuary wherein I cause my name to dwell for three days.[24]

Yadin has discussed the connection between this regulation and that of 1QM 7:6.[25] Yadin notes that the sect interpreted the biblical laws of the camp to refer to the "city of the sanctuary" (עיר המקדש), which, in his view, is the entire city of Jerusalem. B. Levine, on the other hand, has argued that the city of the sanctuary is in fact the temple mount,[26] a view aleady proposed

---

[24] For detailed commentary, see Yadin, *Temple Scroll*, 2. 192–3 and L. H. Schiffman, "Exclusion from the Sanctuary and the City of the Sanctuary in the Temple Scroll," *Biblical and Other Studies in Memory of S. D. Goitein*, Hebrew Annual Review 9 (ed. R. Ahroni; Columbus: Ohio State University, 1985) 301–20. Cf. Lev 22:4. Note that 11QTemple 46:16–18 provides for a special place to the east of the city for those who were impure as a result of seminal emissions. Yadin is correct in taking this to refer to the city of the sanctuary. On the purificatory rites of the *Temple Scroll*, see J. Milgrom, "Studies in the Temple Scroll," *JBL* 97 (1978) 512–18.

[25] See the detailed discussion in Yadin, *Temple Scroll*, 1. 288–89.

[26] B. A. Levine, "The Temple Scroll: Aspects of its Historical Provenance and Literary Character," *BASOR* 232 (1978) 5–23; J. Milgrom, "'Sabbath' and 'Temple City' in the Temple Scroll," *BASOR* 232 (1978) 25–27, and Yadin's response to Levine in "Is the Temple Scroll a Sectarian Document?" *Humanizing America's Iconic Book: Society for Biblical Literature Centennial Addresses 1980* (ed. G. M. Tucker, D. A. Knight; Chico: Scholars Press, 1982) 153–69.

by L. Ginzberg based on the *Zadokite Fragments*.[27] In fact, it was the intention of the author of the *Temple Scroll* to extend the *temenos* to include almost all of what was in his day the city of Jerusalem. This expanded temple enclosure is termed by him עיר המקדש. In any case, we certainly have a similar prescription.

Yadin cites as the basis of the purificatory rituals described here the account of Israel's purification in preparation for the Sinaitic revelation in Exod 19:10–15. This passage also served as the basis for the requirement of purification for the sectarian assembly in the end of days which is described in 1QSa 1:25–27.[28] For our purposes, the passage from the *Temple Scroll* shows that a seminal emission renders a man impure and forbidden to enter the sacred precincts. In the same way, in Yadin's view, such people were enjoined from participating in the battle at the end of days and from the messianic council of the *Rule of the Congregation*.

Yadin considers the *Temple Scroll* to be part of the corpus of documents of the Dead Sea sect. There has been some dispute regarding this matter.[29] If one takes the view that the *Temple Scroll* reflects the work of only a similar and in some way related group and simply was part of the Qumran sect's library, then it is not certain that the sect would have subscribed to all the regulations of this scroll. Nonetheless, the *Temple Scroll* and the other Qumran manuscripts certainly demonstrate the close affinities among the various sectarian circles of the Second Commonwealth.

11QTemple 45:15–18, a few lines after the passage we have just discussed, supplies further information:

וכול איש אשר יטהר מזובו, וספר לו שבעת ימים לטהרתו, ויכבס ביום
השביעי בגדיו, ורחץ את כול בשרו במים חיים. אחר יבוא אל עיר המקדש.
וכול טמא לנפש לוא יבואו לה עד אשר יטהרו. וכול צרוע ומנוגע לוא יבואו
לה עד אשר יטהרו.

And any man who becomes pure from his issue (gonorrhea), shall count for himself seven days for his purification, and launder his clothes on the seventh day, and wash all his flesh in living waters. Afterwards, he may enter the city of the sanctuary. And anyone who is impure by impurity of the dead may not enter it (the city of the sanctuary) until they (*sic*)[30] are purified. And any צרוע and one stricken may not enter it (the city of the sanctuary) until they are purified.[31]

---

[27] L. Ginzberg, *An Unknown Jewish Sect* (New York: Jewish Theological Seminary, 1976) 73–74.

[28] Above, p. 32.

[29] Yadin, *Temple Scroll* 1. 390–99, L. H. Schiffman, *Sectarian Law in the Dead Sea Scrolls, Courts, Testimony and the Penal Code* (Chico: Scholars Press, 1983) 13–14.

[30] The use of כל איש followed by a plural verb in the distributive sense is common in the *Temple Scroll*. See below, p. 48, on 11QTemple 45:12–14.

[31] For detailed commentary, see Yadin, 2. 149–50. Note that the gonorrheac and the one afflicted with צרעת are assigned special places outside of the city of the sanctuary in 11QTemple

This passage enumerates several classes of individuals excluded from the sanctified precincts until they have completed their purification rituals. These include the gonorrheac, one who had contracted the impurity of the dead, one afflicted with the various forms of diseases listed in Leviticus 13, and one who had contracted the skin disease, צרעת, so often and inaccurately translated as "leprosy." These impurities are most probably those termed טמאת בשרו ("uncleanness of his flesh") in the *War Scroll*. These persons are impure by virtue of causes other than that of seminal emission, and they are to observe the laws of purification listed in the Torah before entering the city of the sanctuary. These same people are forbidden even to enter the military camp according to the *War Scroll*.

That the tannaim also forbade those with gonorrhea and צרעת from entering the temple precincts is a foregone conclusion based on the Torah's explicit laws in this regard. Num 5:2–3, as pointed out by Yadin, had required that such people be excluded from the camp.[32] This was taken by the tannaim to prescribe that gonorrhea restricted those afflicted with it from entering the temple precincts. In fact, the tannaim forbade the one afflicted with צרעת from the entire city of Jerusalem.[33] Deut 23:11 had indicated to the tannaim that one who had had a seminal emission was to be excluded from the temple mount.[34] There was no question that all such people could neither serve as priests nor participate in the fulfillment of the commandment of pilgrimage.

The situation is somewhat different regarding one who had contracted the impurity of the dead. Num 5:2 had classed the טמא לנפש (one unclean as a result of contact with a corpse) with the gonorrheac and the person afflicted with צרעת. Yet the tannaim saw this impurity as disqualifying the afflicted only from entry to the temple courtyard (עזרה).[35] Nonetheless, such a person would have been excluded from priestly service and from fulfilling the commandment of pilgrimage to the temple.

46:16–18. Both these classes are assigned similar places outside of all cities according to 11QTemple 48:14–17. Detailed prescriptions regarding the impurity of the dead are spelled out in 11QTemple 48:11–50:9. See the detailed discussion in Yadin, *Temple Scroll*, 1. 321–28 and L. H. Schiffman, "The Impurity of the Dead in the Temple Scroll," to appear in *Archaeology and History in the Dead Sea Scrolls: The New York University Conference in Memory of Yigael Yadin* (ed. L. H. Schiffman; to be published by the American Schools of Oriental Research). Cf. also Lev 22:4.

[32] Yadin, *Temple Scroll*, 1. 291–92.

[33] *Sifre Zuṭa' Naso'* 5:2 (ed. H. S. Horovitz; Jerusalem: Wahrmann, 1966, p. 228); cf. *b. Pesaḥ.* 67a. Yadin, *Temple Scroll*, 1. 292–3 notes that according to Josephus, *J.W.* 5.5.6 §227 and *Ant.* 3.9.3 §261 both classes were forbidden from the city of Jerusalem, and he takes the view that this same regulation was intended by the *Temple Scroll*.

[34] A ברייתא in *b. Pesaḥ.* 68a; *Sifre Devarim* 255 (ed. L. Finkelstein; New York: Jewish Theological Seminary, 1969) 281.

[35] *T. Kelim Bava' Qamma'* 1:8; *Sifre Zuṭa' Naso'* 5:2 (ed. Horovitz, p. 228); cf. Yadin, *Temple Scroll*, 1. 293.

The Exclusion of the Physically Deformed

Several categories of physical deformity disqualify those afflicted with them from participation in the sectarian assembly of the end of days. This entire passage is based on Lev 21:16–24 which requires that the priests serving in the sanctuary not be afflicted with particular deformities or blemishes.

The phrase נכה רגלים, "crippled in the legs," occurs in 2 Sam 4:4. The Targum translates לקי בתרין רגלוהי, "crippled in both legs." Because Jonathan's surviving son was crippled in both legs, he was disqualified from serving as king. This interpretation would suggest that our text refers to one who was crippled in both legs. Despite the use of the root פסח as a description of this condition in 2 Samuel, it is clear that the author of the *Rule of the Congregation*, who uses this term as well, does not consider these two terms to be synonymous. While the phrase נכה (נכאה) ידים, "crippled in the hands," does not occur in the Bible, it is likely that this phrase refers to one who is deprived of the use of both hands.

These two categories of prohibition are clearly derived from the regulation of Lev 21:19 that a priest suffering from a שבר רגל ("fracture of a leg") or a שבר יד ("fracture of a hand") is prohibited from performing the sacrificial service. The problem is that the exact meaning of these terms in the Bible cannot be determined. From the translations of the Vulgate and the Septuagint,[36] and from tannaitic sources,[37] it would appear that the reference is to fractures which have not healed properly and which have left the priest somewhat deformed.[38] If so, the phrases נכה רגלים ("crippled in the legs") and נכה ידים ("crippled in the hands") ought to be similarly interpreted. We have no way of knowing whether the sect would have included in this category similar injuries which were congenital as did the tannaim.

The tannaim had no trouble in distinguishing the פסח ("lame"), whom we will discuss below, from the one suffering the שבר רגל ("fracture of a leg").[39] The former was one who limped, either in one or both legs. The latter, however, was deformed outwardly. In other words, the one with the שבר ("fracture") would be disqualified even if he walked perfectly, whereas the פסח ("lame") was disqualified even if his legs looked normal. If the sect's exegesis made the same distinction as that of the tannaim we could conclude that the נכה רגלים ("crippled in the legs") and ידים ("hands") suffered either in one or both limbs, and that the distinction was that the פסח ("lame")

[36] LXX has σύντριμμα for שבר. Vulgate has *fracto*. On this and the following deformities, cf. Philo *Special Laws*, 1. 80, 81, 117, 118.

[37] Sifra' 'Emor, Parashah 7:11 (ed. I. H. Weiss; Vienna: J. Schlossberg, 1861–62, p. 98c); ברייתות in b. Bek. 45a.

[38] J. Preuss, *Biblical and Talmudic Medicine* (trans. F. Rosner; London: Sanhedrin Press, 1978) 193.

[39] See "חגר," אנציקלופדיה תלמודית 12. 610–12.

walked with a limp whereas the נכה רגלים ("crippled in the legs") was outwardly deformed.

From biblical passages it seems that the עור ("blind") is blind in both
eyes and therefore cannot see at all.[40] One cannot determine how blindness
was defined, but some passages seem to indicate that inability to find one's
way was the decisive factor, not reading as in our society.

Nonetheless, the tannaim interpreted the blindness which is mentioned
in Lev 21:19 as referring even to one blind only in one eye. Indeed, they
widened the meaning of the term עור ("blind") to include those suffering
from other eye ailments and deformities,[41] besides those mentioned in Lev
21:20. We cannot be certain how the sect took this verse, and, therefore, what
the specific definition of the blind man was. It would seem probable, though,
that the sect in its stringency would have interpreted the Torah to exclude
those with the greatest variety of deformities and blemishes from the priestly
service in the temple.

Our list of disqualifications in the *Rule of the Congregation* deviates from
the pattern of Leviticus 21 in including the חרש, "deaf," and אלם, "dumb."
These two categories have been included as a result of Scriptural exegesis
which taught the sect that these two categories were also to be disqualified
from the priestly service. The combination עור ("blind") and פסח ("lame")
occurs in a number of passages, including Lev 21:18. It should be noted that
Deut 15:21 classes עור ("blind") and פסח ("lame") as blemishes which disqualify a first-born animal from sacrifice. The difficult account of 2 Sam 5:6–8
relates that when David attacked Jerusalem, the Jebusites taunted him and
said that the blind and the lame would turn back his advance. In com-
memoration of his victory, it was said, presumably at a later date, that the
blind and the lame may not enter the temple (הבית). This passage must have
greatly influenced our text. The primary basis for the sect's views, however,
was Exod 4:11 which links the עור ("blind") with the אלם ("dumb") and חרש
("deaf"). The sect reasoned, basing itself on this passage, that the same disqualification applied to the חרש ("deaf") and אלם ("dumb") as applied to the
עור ("blind") in Lev 21:18.[42]

The nominal use of חרש ("deaf") in the Bible makes it clear that it
designates one who does not hear.[43] In other words, both ears do not function.
The biblical deaf person was often unable to speak since he had been deaf
from early childhood. This is how a root which normally means "to be silent"
could be the basis of a noun describing a deaf person. Tannaitic opinion
recognized two kinds of חרש ("deaf [person]"). One type neither hears nor

---

[40] Lev 19:14, Deut 27:18, 28:29, Isa 42:18, 59:10, Job 29:15. On blindness in biblical and rabbinic literature, see Preuss, *Medicine*, 270–76.

[41] *Sifra' 'Emor, Parashah* 3:5 (ed. Weiss, p. 95b), ברייתא in *b. Bek.* 44a.

[42] Cf. Carmignac, *Textes*, 2. 23, n. 65.

[43] Ps 38:14, Isa 29:18, 42:18.

speaks, and is, therefore, considered legally incompetent. This person was congenitally deaf and therefore never learned to speak. The second is one who is deaf but does speak. Such a person had learned to speak before becoming deaf.[44]

Tannaitic halakhah disqualified the חרש ("deaf") from performing the priestly service in the temple.[45] While it is most probable that this refers to one who neither speaks nor hears, some later traditional scholars think it might have applied also to one who could speak but could not hear.[46] Further, the חרש ("deaf") was exempt from the obligation of pilgrimage to the temple on the three festivals.[47] This appears to refer only to the one who neither speaks nor hears and who, therefore, is mentally incompetent.[48] Nevertheless, some tannaim understood this exemption to include those who could speak but could not hear (as well as those who could hear but could not speak). Some amoraim ruled that one who was deaf even in one ear was exempted from this commandment.[49] It is difficult to determine from these parallels how far the sect might have gone in its disqualifications. It should again be emphasized that the sect's desire to ensure ultimate perfection and purity might have led them to exclude even the most minimally unfit.

The term אלם ("dumb") in the Bible denotes one who cannot speak.[50] The tannaim understood this to refer to one who heard but could not speak.[51] In other words, such a person was physically unable to speak, as opposed to the type of חרש ("deaf") who could not speak as a result of his inability to hear. Some tannaim ruled that such persons were exempt from the requirement of pilgrimage on the three festivals.[52] The sect learned from Exod 4:11 that the אלם ("dumb"), like the עור ("blind"), was to be excluded from priestly service, and, hence, from participation in the eschatological council.

The term מנוגע ("afflicted") occurs four times in our text from the *Rule of the Congregation*. The first occurrence (line 3), as we have already seen, refers to those stricken with forms of ritual impurity. The second (line 4) is in a general statement which introduces the list of disqualifications due to physical deformity. The third (line 5) and fourth (line 6) refer to various types of blemishes, termed מומים by the Bible and the rabbis. The first of these

---

[44] *M. Ter.* 1:2, *t. Ter.* 1:2, and the detailed discussion in A. J. Peck, *The Priestly Gift in Mishnah* (Chico: Scholars Press, 1981) 30–37. Cf. *b. Ḥag.* 2b, *b. Giṭ.* 71a and "חרש," אנציקלופדיה תלמודית 17. 495–99.

[45] *M. Bek.* 7:6; *Sifra' 'Emor, Pereq* 3:2 (ed. Weiss, p. 95c).

[46] "חרש," 536.

[47] *M. Ḥag.* 1:1.

[48] This view is supported by the occurrence of the grouping חרש, שוטה, וקטן in this mishnah.

[49] *B. Ḥag.* 2b-3a, *y. Ḥag.* 1:1 (75d-76a). Cf. D. Halivni, מקורות ומסורות, סדר מועד (Jerusalem: Jewish Theological Seminary, 1974–75) 575–77.

[50] Exod 4:11, Isa 35:6, Ps 38:14.

[51] See above, n. 44.

[52] See above, n. 49

types of blemishes is referred to by the phrase מנוגע [בבשרו] ("afflicted in his flesh"). This phrase clearly represents an exegesis of the phrase אשר בו מום ("who has a blemish in him") in Lev 21:17. Our text uses בבשרו ("in his flesh") as an explanation of the Bible's בו ("in him"), which was somewhat vague. One afflicted with such a condition, in the view of the sectarians, was prohibited not only from performing the priestly service in the Jerusalem temple, but also from participating in the sectarian eschatological assembly.

Some tannaim did, however, accord certain subsidiary priestly privileges to priests with blemishes.[53] While the tannaim differentiated the permanent blemish (מום קבוע) from the temporary blemish (מום עובר), they understood this verse to refer to both.[54] This seems to be the interpretation of the sect. In lines 7–8 the *Rule of the Congregation* excludes also one afflicted with a blemish in his flesh "visible to the eyes" (לראות עינים). This phraseology exactly matches that of the tannaim, but it seems that the meaning of the usages in the two literatures is not the same. To the tannaim, certain conditions prohibited those afflicted from performing the priestly service מפני מראית העין ("because of the sight of the eye").[55] The exact meaning of this phrase is itself difficult. The correct view seems to be that these people were excluded because of the unattractiveness of these conditions.[56] To the tannaim, these were not conditions which the Torah had excluded. To the sect, though, the phrase לראות עינים ("visible to the eyes") designated those afflicted with temporary blemishes, those termed מום עובר by the tannaim. Both the tannaim and the sect took the view that the Torah had prohibited priests with these conditions from performing the temple service. The sect saw such people as excluded from the eschatological council of the community as well.

A parallel to our passage may be cited from 1QM 7:4. Among those who are excluded from participation in the eschatological battle are:

> ... וכול פסח או עור, או חגר או איש אשר מום עולם בבשרו.

> ... every lame man or blind man, or cripple or a man who has a permanent blemish in his flesh.

This passage is extremely helpful for the interpretation of our text, since many of the same people are disqualified in both lists. The חגר ("cripple") of the *War Scroll* is the נכה רגלים ("crippled in the legs") of the *Rule of the Congregation* who has an improperly healed fracture which leaves him

---

[53] ברייתא in *b. Yoma* 23b; *t. Soṭa* 7:16; *Sifre Be-Midbar* 75 (ed. Horovitz, p. 70), and parallels in S. Lieberman, תוספתא כפשוטה (New York: Jewish Theological Seminary, 1955–) 7. 682, commentary to lines 132–4. Cf. "בעל מום," אנציקלופדיה תלמודית, 4. 115–17.

[54] *Sifra' 'Emor, Parashah* 3:5 (ed. Weiss, p. 95b); cf. *m. Bek.* 7:1, *t. Bek.* 5:1, and J. Neusner, *A History of the Mishnaic Law of Holy Things* (Leiden: E. J. Brill, 1979) 3. 199, 203.

[55] *M. Bek.* 7:3 and 5, *t. Bek.* 5:2. Cf. Neusner, *Holy Things*, 3. 200–1, 203.

[56] So I. Lipschutz, תפארת ישראל, in *Mishnah* (New York: Pardes, 1952–53) to *m. Bek.* 7:3. Cf. Licht, מגילת הסרכים, 265.

deformed. Even if he walks properly, his presence will in some way defile the military camp, so he may not go to war. The lame (פסח), as above, is the one who limps, even if his limbs are formed properly. Such a person, not only for practical military reasons, but also for reasons of sanctity, cannot go to war with the armies of the sect. In regard to these deformities, the sect has the same requirements for the eschatological council as it has for the battles of the end of days. The correspondence has led J. Carmignac to suggest that the *War Scroll* version is dependent on that of the *Rule of the Congregation*.[57] Yet in regard to blemishes, the laws are not the same. Only a permanent blemish disqualifies one from battle, while even a temporary blemish would prevent participation in the council of the community at the end of days.

Some note should be taken of the usage of חגר ("cripple") in tannaitic texts. The tannaim encountered difficulty in differentiating the פסח ("lame") from the חגר ("cripple") and various later commentators have offered explanations.[58] Suffice it to say that the חגר ("cripple") was exempted from the commandment of pilgrimage.[59] An amora took this law as applying even if his condition was only in one leg,[60] and priests with this condition were disqualified from priestly service.[61] We have already seen how the sect distinguished these two categories.

The passage from the *War Scroll* makes no mention of the blind, those with a fractured arm which has healed improperly, the deaf and the dumb. While it is most likely that such people were not intended to go to war with the sect, this is not stated explicitly. It is even possible that the author of the *War Scroll* did not see the deaf and dumb as excluded by the law of purity since he did not make the connection with Exod 4:11 that we have suggested above.

There is also a parallel to our passage in CD 15:15-17. This passage is extremely fragmentary in the medieval manuscripts. J. T. Milik has identified a manuscript of this text from cave 4 which has been given the siglum 4QDb. Milik has suggested the following restored translation,[62] without publishing the text:

Fools, madmen (*mšwg'*), simpletons and imbeciles (*mšwgh*), the blind (lit., those who, being weak of eye, cannot see), the maimed (*ḥgr*), the

---

[57] Carmignac, *Textes* 1. 103, n. 7; idem, *Règle*, 105.

[58] See "חגר," אנציקלופדיה תלמודית, 12. 610-12.

[59] M. Ḥag. 1:2.

[60] B. Ḥag. 3a.

[61] *Sifra' 'Emor, Parashah* 3:7 (ed. Weiss, p. 95b) which takes tannaitic Hebrew חגר as equivalent to biblical פסח. Indeed, the Targumim translate פסח as חגיר. According to the *Sifra'*, a priest is disqualified even if he is a חגר in only one leg. Cf. *Sifre Be-Midbar* 75 (ed. H. S. Horovitz; Jerusalem: Bamberger and Wahrmann, 1966, p. 70); *y. Meg.* 1:10 (ed. Krotoschin; 12, 72b).

[62] J. T. Milik, *Ten Years of Discovery in the Wilderness of Judaea* (London: SCM Press, 1959) 114; cf. Licht, מגילת הסרכים, 264. Perhaps correct the transliteration to *wšwgh*.

lame, the deaf, and minors, none of these may enter the midst of the community, for the holy angels (are in the midst of it).

Now this passage must be compared with our listing. It seems to us that the
initial mention of the fools and madmen is actually the end of the previous
sentence, as can be shown from comparison with the medieval fragments in
our possession. The remaining designations are the subject of the prohibition.
While Milik sees this text as excluding the classes of people listed from
entrance to the sect, comparison with our text and the conclusions to be
reached below would recommend a different interpretation. Most probably,
this text, upon publication, will be seen to refer to entrance into the assembly
of the sect, a privilege denied to those listed. This passage is certainly referring to the present age. Indeed, all those prohibited from the eschatological
assembly are the very same ones who could not attend the מושב הרבים (the
sectarian assembly) in the present, for in the present the sect lived in such
a way as to emulate and prepare for the way of life of the end of days. Detailed
analysis of this passage, however, will have to await its publication in the
original Hebrew.

A partial parallel to the disqualification of the deformed may also be
cited from 11QTemple 45:12–14:

כול איש עור לוא יבואו לה כול ימיהמה ולוא יטמאו את העיר אשר אני שוכן
בתוכה. כי אני ה׳ שוכן בתוך בני ישראל לעולם ועד.

> No blind man may enter it (the city of the sanctuary) for their (*sic*) entire
> life so that they will not render impure the city in which I dwell. For I am
> the Lord Who dwells among the children of Israel for ever.[63]

This passage is found in the *Temple Scroll* immediately after the excerpt
quoted above. It prohibits the blind from entering the sacred precincts. Yadin
has already noted that this passage is based on Lev 21:18. He suggests that
the actual meaning of the passage is that all of the deformities listed in the
Leviticus passage disqualify the subject from entry into the city of the sanctuary; mention of the blind man functions here only as an example.[64]

It is difficult to maintain that the material dealing with the other deformities has been omitted by scribal error from our manuscript of the *Temple
Scroll*, since a second fragment apparently preserves the very same text.[65] It
is possible to propose an alternate restoration for the fragment so that it
would include one or two additional deformities, but Yadin's restoration in
light of the 11Q manuscript of the complete scroll is certainly most probable.
Yet it is difficult to see how the word עור, "blind man," could have been used

---

[63] For commentary, see Yadin, *Temple Scroll*, 2. 193. Note that the scroll makes no provisions
for special places in which to quarantine the blind or any other deformed individuals, neither
for the city of the sanctuary nor other cities.

[64] See his detailed discussion in Yadin, *Temple Scroll*, 1. 289–90 and 2. 193.

[65] Rockefeller 43.976, in Yadin, *Temple Scroll*, 2. 188–9.

as a general term by the author of the *Temple Scroll*. It is more likely that the omission of the other deformities found in Leviticus 21 from the *Temple Scroll* is to be explained as an oversight of the author(s).[66]

The Aged

Our passage also excludes from the council an elder who stumbles so as not to be able to take his stand in the assembly. The absence of the technical use of the root כשל ("stumble") in the Bible makes the precise definition of this term difficult on philological grounds.[67] Indeed, the usual usage of this verb in biblical literature is to designate moral or religious stumbling. Only comparison of this regulation with similar prescriptions in other Qumran texts will avail. We have already seen in Chapter One that 1QSa 1:19–20 expects the role of the sectarian in the affairs of the sect to decrease as he attains old age. Several passages make clear that to the sect, the age of sixty was the appropriate age for retirement from serving as judge, military leader, or sectarian official.

In view of the parallels regarding judicial and military service, all of which were discussed in detail in Chapter One, it seems that the איש זקן כושל ("the elder who stumbles") is one who has passed the age of sixty years. From that age on he is not to be allowed to take a stand among the council of the community. For the sect, apparently, priests were to cease their service at the age of sixty. This is probably another correspondence between the law for disqualification from the priesthood and that of entry into the eschatological council of the sect.

Tannaitic law provides that the זקן ("elder") is exempt from the commandment of pilgrimage.[68] Such an elder is undoubtedly to be understood as one who has grown too old to be able to walk sufficiently well to make the pilgrimage.[69] It is possible that this definition ought to be applied to the "tottering old man" of the *Rule of the Congregation*.

The Presence of the Angels

Our text gives a specific reason for its requirements of purity, absence of those with specific deformities, and the aged. According to the *Rule of the*

---

[66] Note that according to Matt 21:14, Jesus healed the blind and the lame in the temple. Cf. Luke 14:21.

[67] Note that in Dan 11:35 this verb occurs with משכילים, a term which was used by the sect to refer to those who had achieved high standards of both scholarship and conduct. Cf. L. H. Schiffman, *Halakhah at Qumran* (Leiden: E. J. Brill, 1975) 25, n. 24.

[68] M. Ḥag. 1:1.

[69] M. Maimonides, פרוש המשניות (ed. J. Kafah; Jerusalem: Mosad Harav Kook, 1963) *ad loc.* and idem, *Mishneh Torah* (Jerusalem: Pardes, 1955), *Hilkhot Ḥagigah* 2:1. To the tannaim, the requirement was only that one be able to make the trip from the city of Jerusalem to the temple mount by foot.

Congregation, the angels are regarded as being in the assembly.[70] 1QM 7:6 gives the very same reason for the requirement that those impure from a seminal emission not participate in the eschatological battle:

כיא מלאכי קודש עם צבאותם יחד.

For holy angels are together with their armies.[71]

B. M. Bokser suggests that this is actually a reworking of Deut 23:15 that explains the requirement of ritual purity in the military camp as resulting from the presence of the Lord. Bokser maintains that the divine presence is represented here by the angels.[72]

A parallel to this very concept occurs in 1QM 12:7–8 where it is stated that the angels are fighting among the members of the sect:

כי קדוש אדוני, ומלך הכבוד אתנו. עם קדושים, גבורים וצבא מלאכים
בפקודינו, וגבור המלח[נמה] בעדתנו, וצבא רוחיו עם צעדינו.

For the Lord is holy, and the King of Glory is with us. A people of holy ones, her[oes and] a host of angels is mustered with us, and the Mighty One of w[ar] is in our congregation, and the host of His spirits marches with us (lit. "is with our steps").[73]

It was a cardinal belief of the sect that just as the world below is divided into the domains of the two spirits, those of good and evil, so was the world of the angels. Just as the teacher of righteousness and the wicked priest represented the forces of good and evil to the sect in the present age, so the Prince of Light (the angel Michael) and his enemy, Belial, represented the very same forces on high. These forces would be arrayed against each other in the end of days, just as they are in the present pre-messianic age.[74]

The great eschatological battle would be fought, therefore, both in heaven and on earth. The actual battle would be a simultaneous and mutual one, in which the angels and men would fight side by side. After the long series of engagements described in the *War Scroll,* the forces of good would be victorious. For this reason the sect believed that in the end of days the angels would be present in the military camp described in the *War Scroll.*

---

[70] The same idea appears in 1QH 6:13. For a New Testament parallel, cf. J. A. Fitzmyer, "A Feature of Qumran Angelology and the Angels of 1 Cor 11:10," *Essays on the Semitic Background of the New Testament* (London: Geoffrey Chapman, 1974) 187–204. Fitzmyer discusses the Qumran material on 198–99.

[71] Cf. the reading of 4Q491 (M^a), כי מלאכי קודש במערכותמה (Baillet, DJD 7. 13).

[72] Bokser, "Approaching Sacred Space," 283.

[73] The translation has been adapted from that in Yadin, *War Scroll,* 317. See the commentaries of Yadin, Carmignac and Jongeling for complete philological notes.

[74] Yadin, *War Scroll,* 229–42; J. Licht, "An Analysis of the Treatise of the Two Spirits in DSD," *Aspects of the Dead Sea Scrolls* (Scripta Hierosolymitana 4; ed. C. Rabin and Y. Yadin; Jerusalem: Magnes Press, 1958) 87–100. The same idea is found in 1QS 11:8 (Barthélemy, DJD, 1. 117).

At the same time, the eschatological council would also involve both the earthly and heavenly sons of light.

The appearance of the very same reason for the prohibitions in our text from the *Rule of the Congregation* and in the *War Scroll* may allow another important conclusion. 1QM 7:3–4 provides that women and children are to be excluded from the military camp:[75]

וכול נער זעטוט ואשה לוא יבואו למחנותם בצאתם מירושלים ללכת למלחמה עד שובם.

No young boy[76] or woman shall enter their encampments when they go forth from Jerusalem to go to battle until they return.

It is most likely that the very same regulation was in force regarding the eschatological council. Although women and children would be part of the sect, as is evident from 1QSa 1:6–11, their presence among the angels in the council of the community would not be allowed, as it was not in the military camp of the battle for the end of days.[77]

Deposition by the Disqualified

That those disqualified from the eschatological council were still expected to be part of the sect in the end of days can be seen from the last prescription of our text. It indicates that if one of those disqualified from the council wished to present a matter for consideration by that body, it was to be done by deposition. The text does not indicate who would take the deposition, but it is to be assumed that some official, perhaps the מבקר ("examiner"), would discharge this function. This passage most probably provides insight into the conduct of the sect in the present age as well. Apparently, in the everyday life of the sect, those who were impure or disqualified for reasons of physical deformity were not permitted into the מושב הרבים (the sectarian assembly). Such people, however, could be members of the sect and were allowed representation by deposition. Such deposition was given to the מבקר ("examiner") who then presented it before the sectarian assembly. In this way the opportunity was granted for all members of the sect to be heard in the assembly, without compromising the all-important requirement of ritual purity and perfection of the highest level. Indeed, this seems to be the ruling of CD 14:11–12 for the present age:

ולכל דבר אשר יהיה לכל האדם לדבר למבקר, ידבר לכל ריב ומשפט.

---

[75] Trans. in Yadin, *War Scroll*, 291.

[76] Yadin notes that this refers to a boy below the age of twenty-five. Cf. 1QSa 1:12 and Schiffman, *Sectarian Law*, 30–32. On זעטוט, see Yadin, *War Scroll*, 290.

[77] According to Yadin, the *Temple Scroll* envisages that no woman will be permitted to live in the city of the sanctuary, taken by him as Jerusalem (Yadin, *Temple Scroll*, 1. 237).

And regarding any matter about which any man has to speak to the
examiner, let him speak regarding any (legal) case or judgment.[78]

Those who could not consult the council, the מושב הרבים, in the present
age would give depositions to the examiner. Only in this manner could such
individuals' petitions or questions be considered. Once again, we have seen
that the life of the sect in the present was to mirror its legislation for the end
of days.

[78] Cf. the similar phraseology in 1QS 6:9–10.

4

THE MESSIANIC BANQUET

The Meal of the End of Days

The Dead Sea sect envisaged an eschatological meal at which the priestly "messiah" would join the messiah of Israel in eating bread and wine amidst the entire congregation of Israel. The messianic banquet is described in 1QSa 2:11–22:[1]

[מוֹ]שַׁב אַנְשֵׁי הַשֵּׁם [קְרִיאֵי] מוֹעֵד לַעֲצַת הַיַּחַד אִם יוֹ[תוֹעֵ]ד [בְּעֵת קֵץ] הַמָּשִׁיחַ
אִתָּם. יָבוֹא [הַכֹּהֵן] בְּ[רֹא]שׁ כֹּל עֲדַת יִשְׂרָאֵל, וְכֹל אֶחָיו בְּנֵי אַהֲרֹן הַכֹּהֲנִים
[קְרִיאֵי] מוֹעֵד אֲנֹשֵׁי הַשֵּׁם, וְיָשְׁבוּ לְ[פְנָיו אִישׁ] לְפִי כְבוֹדוֹ. וְאַחַר [יָבוֹא מְשִׁי]חַ
יִשְׂרָאֵל וְיָשְׁבוּ לְפָנָיו רָאשֵׁי [אַלְפֵי יִשְׂרָאֵל אִי]שׁ לְפִי כְבוֹדוֹ, כְּ[נ]מְעַמְדוֹ
בְמַחֲנֵיהֶם וּבְמַסָּעֵיהֶם. וְכֹל רָאשֵׁי [אֲבוֹת הָעֵדָ]ה עִם חַכְמֵיהֶם וִידָעֵיהֶם יֵשְׁבוּ
לִפְנֵיהֶם אִישׁ לְפִי כְבוֹדוֹ. וְ[אִם לַשֻּׁלְחָן] יַחַד יוֹעֵדוּ לָשִׂים לֶחֶם וְתִי[רוֹשׁ, וְעָרוּ]ךְ
הַשֻּׁלְחָן הַיַּחַד [לְאֱכוֹל וְהַ]תִירוֹשׁ לִשְׁתּוֹ[ת, אַל] יִשְׁלַח אִישׁ אֶת יָדוֹ בְּרֵשִׁית
הַלֶּחֶם וְהַתִּירוֹ[שׁ] לִפְנֵי הַכֹּהֵן. כִּי[א] הוֹאָה יְבָרֵךְ אֶת רֵשִׁית הַלֶּחֶם וְהַתִּירוֹ[שׁ
וְיִשְׁלַח] יָדוֹ בַּלֶּחֶם לְפָנִים. וְאַחַר יִשְׁלַ[ח] מְשִׁיחַ יִשְׂרָאֵל יָדָיו בַּלֶּחֶם. וְ[אַחַר
יְבָרְ]כוּ כֹּל עֲדַת הַיַּחַד, אִ[ישׁ] לְפִ[י] כְבוֹדוֹ. וּכְחוּק הַזֶּה יַעֲשׂוֹ[ן] לְכוֹל מַעֲרֶכֶת
כִּי יִוָּעֵדוּ עַד עִשְׂרָא אֲנָשִׁי[ם].

[The ses]sion[2] of the men of renown, [invited to] the feast[3] for the council

---

[1] Restorations are with J. Licht, מגילת הסרכים (Jerusalem: Bialik Institute, 1965) 269–70. See also the studies of E. F. Sutcliffe, "The Rule of the Congregation (1QSa), II, 11–12: Text and Meaning," *RQ* 2 (1959–60) 541–47; Y. Yadin, "A Crucial Passage in the Dead Sea Scrolls," *JBL* 78 (1959) 238–41; M. Smith, "God's Begetting the Messiah in 1QSa," *NTS* 5 (1958/9) 218–24; J. F. Priest, "The Messiah and the Meal in 1QSa," *JBL* 82 (1963) 95–100; R. Gordis, "The 'Begotten' Messiah in the Qumran Scrolls," *VT* 7 (1957) 191–194; and K. G. Kuhn, "The Lord's Supper and the Communal Meal at Qumran," *The Scrolls and the New Testament* (ed. K. Stendahl; London: SCM Press, 1958) 70–72.

[2] Barthélemy (D. Barthélemy and J. T. Milik, *Qumran Cave I*, Discoveries in the Judaean Desert 1 [Oxford: Clarendon Press, 1962] 110) and Sutcliffe ("Rule," 541) restore [זה מוֹ]שַׁב, which, as Licht notes, is too large for the space (מגילת הסרכים, 269). Carmignac also notes that the space is too small (J. Carmignac, "Quelques détails de lecture," *RQ* 4 [1963–64] 85 and idem, "La Règle de la congrégation," *Les textes de Qumran* [ed. J. Carmignac, É. Cothenet and H. Lignée; Paris: Letouzey et Ané, 1963] 2. 24). He restores [לְמוֹ]שַׁב, taking the first sentence of our text as belonging to the previous paragraph. He begins our passage with אִם (line 11). Nonetheless, Licht has shown that it is still preferable to take this clause as the heading for what follows (מגילת הסרכים, 269).

[3] Translating with F. M. Cross, *The Ancient Library at Qumran* (Garden City, New York:

of the community when [at the end][4] (of days) the messiah[5] [shall assemble][6]
with them. [The priest][7] shall enter [at] the head of all the congregation of
Israel, and [all his brethren the sons of][8] Aaron, the priests, [who are
invited] to the feast, the men of renown,[9] and they shall sit be[fore him,
each][10] according to his importance. Afterwards,[11] [the messiah] of Israel
[shall enter][12] and the heads[13] of the [thousands of Israel][14] shall sit before
him [ea]ch according to his importance, according to [his station] in their
encampments and their journeys.[15] And all of the heads of the [households

---

Doubleday, 1961) 87 and n. 65. קראי מועד אנשי שם appears in Num 16:2 as a description of
the princes of the congregation who joined Korah, Dathan, Abiram, and On in their rebellion
against Moses and Aaron.

[4] On the significance of קץ at Qumran, see H. Yalon, מגילות מדבר יהודה (Jerusalem: Shrine
of the Book Fund and Kiryath Sepher, 1967) 77.

[5] Here referring to the messiah of Israel. On the two messiahs, see below n. 32.

[6] Accepting the restoration of Licht. For the proposed restorations, see Licht, מגילת הסרכים,
267–69, J. Maier, *Die Texte vom Toten Meer* (Munich and Basel: Ernst Reinhardt, 1960) 2. 158–59,
and Cross, *Ancient Library*, 87–88, n. 67. The numerous textual problems and restorations in
this entire passage in no way affect the basic conclusions reached below. Note, however, that P.
Skehan calls "on the testimony of a half-dozen witnesses, including Allegro, Cross, Strugnell, and
the writer [Skehan], as of the summer of 1955," to the effect that the text "contains *yolid*," i.e.
that this is the correct reading of the MS ("Two Books on Qumran Studies," *CBQ* 21 [1959] 74).

[7] Barthélemy (DJD 1. 110) restored [הכוהן], with no preposition. See Licht, מגילת הסרכים,
267 for other restorations. To be added to Licht's list is the suggestion of Sutcliffe ("Rule," 541),
[וגם הוא בראש]. This suggestion is rendered unlikely by the continuation of the passage which
speaks about a priestly figure.

[8] Restored with Licht (following traces) who compares 1QM 15:4. Licht also suggests restoring [ונועדו אליו], but it is difficult to see how this would connect with the continuation of the
text (מגילת הסרכים, 269). Perhaps he meant to suggest [ונועדו אליו בני]. While such a restoration would make sense, it would be too long for the space available. Barthélemy restored אבות
[בני] (DJD 1. 110). Carmignac apparently prefers [אחיו בני], and compares 1 Chr 16:39, Neh 3:1,
and 1QM 13:1, 15:4 ("Quelques détails," 85–86 and "Règle," 24).

[9] The form אנושי (also in 1QSa 1:28) is a construct of אנוש, here substituted for the biblical
אנשי encountered in line 11. The ו is serving for Masoretic קמץ קטן. קמץ השם אנשי (with definite
article) occurs in Gen 6:4. Rashi's comment to this verse raises the possibility that our passage
here may refer to those whose names appear in the official roster of the members of the sect.
Cf. *Tg. Ps.-J.* to Num 16:2, מפרשין בשמהן. On the sectarian rosters, see L. Schiffman, *Halakhah
at Qumran* (Leiden: E. J. Brill, 1975) 66–67.

[10] For the restorations, cf. lines 15–17 and 1:18.

[11] The adverbial usage is noted by Licht, מגילת הסרכים, 269.

[12] Barthélemy restored ישב משיח (DJD 1. 110). The י is suspended above the line.

[13] The י is suspended above the line.

[14] Part of the א of אלפי is visible. Cf. 1QSa 1:14 (Licht, מגילת הסרכים, 269). Carmignac
restores [שבטי ישראל] with 1 Sam 15:17 ("Règle," 25).

[15] Barthélemy emends to ובמעשיהם (DJD 1. 118). Licht and Carmignac note the mention
of the system of encampment and march in Num 9:15–10:34 (Licht, מגילת הסרכים, 269;
Carmignac, "Règle," 25). The organization of Israel in the desert period greatly influenced the
sect and its view of the messianic era. See Yadin, *The Scroll of the War of the Sons of Light against
the Sons of Darkness* (Oxford: Oxford University Press, 1962) 38–64 and S. Talmon, "The 'Desert
Motif' in the Bible and Qumran Literature," *Biblical Motifs* (ed. A. Altmann; Cambridge:
Harvard University Press, 1966) 55–63. The Therapeutae also sat in order of importance

of the congrega]tion,[16] [their] sag[es and wise men,][17] shall sit before them, each according to his importance. [When they] mee[t[18] at the] communal[19] [tab]le,[20] [to set out bread and wi]ne,[21] and the communal table is arranged [to eat and][22] to dri[nk] wine, [no] one [shall extend] his hand to the first (portion)[23] of the bread and [the wine] before[24] the priest. Fo[r he shall] bless[25] the first (portion) of the bread and the win[e and shall extend][26] his hand to the bread first.[27] Afterwa[rds,] the messiah of Israel [shall exten]d his hands to the bread. [Afterwards,] all of the congregation of the community [shall ble]ss, ea[ch according to] his importance.[28] [They] shall act[29] according to this statute whenever (the meal) is ar[ranged][30] when as many as ten[31] [meet] together.

The banquet described in our text is presided over by the two messianic figures expected by the sectarians.[32] These were the priest, under whose administration and direction the cult would be restored in the "New

---

according to Philo *Contemplative Life* 67. Cf. also Matt 23:6 and Luke 14:7–11 on the "place of honor" at the table (Carmignac, "Règle," 26).

[16] Traces of the first and last letters are visible. Cf. 1QSa 1:24–25 which is also partly restored.

[17] Restored with Licht who notes that half of the first מ is visible and compares 1QSa 1:28 (מגילת הסרכים, 269). Barthélemy restored חכמי עדת הקודש] (DJD 1. 111). On Licht's restoration, cf. Deut 1:13 that requires that our text as restored be vocalized וִידָעֵיהֶם. While Rashi, Ibn Ezra, and Nahmanides all take ידעים to refer to men of reputation, we have translated here in accord with *Tg. Ps.-J.* מרי מנדעא, "men of knowledge."

[18] נפעל of יעד, "to meet at an appointed place" (BDB, 416).

[19] Taking יחד here as a designation of the sect. Alternately, one can translate, "[at the tab]le together."

[20] Part of the ה is visible.

[21] Barthélemy restored]או לשתות הת[יִרוש (DJD, 1. 111).

[22] Barthélemy restored]ומסוך ה[תירוש (DJD, 1. 111). Cf. Prov 9:2.

[23] The word ברשת may be taken as either an adverb modifying the verb ישלח (he should not take his bread or wine first) or a noun meaning the first portion, as translated here. Cf. P. Wernberg-Møller, *The Manual of Discipline* (Leiden: E. J. Brill, 1957) 103.

[24] Written over an erasure.

[25] Barthélemy restores כיא הוא מ]בֶרך (DJD 1. 111).

[26] Barthélemy restores ושלח (DJD 1. 111).

[27] Cf. Ruth 4:7. Licht notes that in this and other biblical texts the word does not make reference to any specific time. A usage closer to that of our text is found in Ben Sira 4:17, 11:8, 37:8 (מגילת הסרכים, 270). 1QS 6:5 (below, pp. 57–58) uses לרישונה in the same sense.

[28] Licht observes that each would recite his own benediction, a practice in opposition to that of the tannaim (מגילת הסרכים, 270).

[29] Barthélemy and Licht suggest that the ו may have been suspended above the line.

[30] Barthélemy compares 1QS 10:14.

[31] For the spelling with final א, cf. תורא in 1QSa 1:11 (above, p. 18), and Licht, מגילת הסרכים, 257.

[32] See the sources cited in Schiffman, *Halakhah at Qumran*, 51, n. 202 as well as R. E. Brown, "The Messianism of Qumran," *CBQ* 19 (1957) 163–75; K. G. Kuhn, "The Two Messiahs of Aaron and Israel," *The Scrolls and the New Testament* (ed. K. Stendahl; London: SCM Press, 1958) 54–64; Priest, "The Messiah and the Meal," 95–100; and L. H. Schiffman, "Messianic Figures and Ideas in the Qumran Scrolls," to appear in *The Messiah* (ed. J. H. Charlesworth; Anchor Bible Reference Library; Garden City: Doubleday).

Jerusalem," and the messiah of Israel who would serve as the temporal and military leader. In keeping with the importance of the priesthood at Qumran and the emphasis placed upon the restoration of the purified cult in the days to come, the priestly "messiah" is given the higher position.

The eschatological banquet is to be eaten seated, as opposed to the tannaitic usage of reclining at formal meals. Indeed, reclining was the Greco-Roman pattern, whereas the biblical tradition was one of sitting. The messianic banquet, in keeping with the approach of the sect, would embody the traditions of Israel, not those of the Hellenistic pagans.

The foods mentioned here are bread and wine. While these probably did not constitute the entire menu, they are singled out since only these two benedictions must be recited at the eschatological meal. The benediction over bread covered the other foods as well, except for the wine brought to the table during the meal which required its own benediction. Whereas the communal meal of the sect as described in 1QS 6:2–5 required *either* bread or wine, the messianic banquet would involve both. The priest would recite the benediction first and receive the first portion of the bread and wine. All others present would recite the benediction in the order of their rank after the priestly messiah. The meals require the quorum of ten men.

The requirement of absolute physical purity had to be in force for the messianic banquet. 1QSa 2:3–9 indicates that those with physical imperfections were to be excluded from the "congregation" in the end of days.

The ultimate perfection of the messianic era would be the realization of the sect's constant striving for total ritual purity. Therefore, total ritual purity may be seen as a catalyst which turns the ordinary communal meal into a foretaste of the great messianic banquet at the end of days.

The Sectarian Communal Meal

Whereas the messianic banquet of rabbinic sources was to be a one-time affair inaugurating the messianic era,[33] the Dead Sea community looked forward to a regular series of such banquets to be held in the days to come.[34] The practice of acting out the future messianic banquet by the sect in their everyday lives, to be discussed below, bespeaks the messianic overtones with which their frequent communal meals were invested.

---

[33] On this banquet, see L. Ginzberg, *The Legends of the Jews* (Philadelphia: Jewish Publication Society, 1958) 1. 27–28, 5. 43–46, n. 127, and G.F. Moore, *Judaism* (New York: Schocken, 1971) 2. 363–4. Note that most of the sources cited are considerably later than the Qumran corpus. The numerous apocryphal and pseudepigraphical references to this banquet are conveniently listed in the index to R. H. Charles, *The Apocrypha and Pseudepigrapha of the Old Testament* (Oxford: Clarendon Press, 1913) 2. 859, *s.v.* "Messianic banquet." There can be no question that this idea was widespread when the Qumran texts were composed.

[34] Priest, "Messiah and Meal," 97.

The *Manual of Discipline* alludes to the communal meal of the present age. According to 1QS 6:2–3, wherever members of the group reside:

ויחד יואכלו ויחד יברכו ויחד יועצו.

Together they shall eat; together they shall bless; and together[35] they shall take counsel.

While this passage clearly indicates that communal meals were to be a part of the activities of the sect, it gives no specific information regarding them. There is no mention here of how often such meals should occur or whether all or only some meals were to be taken communally.[36]

Further, the actions described here — eating, blessing, and taking counsel — are independent of one another. The community had various gatherings to fulfill each purpose. Blessing was apparently part of a fixed regimen of daily prayers such as those now available from cave 4.[37] The blessing in the passage under consideration does not refer to the blessings recited for eating food, but rather to the liturgical worship of the group.[38] Taking counsel occurred in the מושב הרבים, the Qumran legislative and judicial assembly.[39] What, then, was the particular nature of the gathering at which the sectarians partook of a communal meal?

In 1QS 6:3–4 the text specifies that wherever there are ten members of the group, there must always be a priest. As in the messianic banquet, the members shall sit before him according to rank, and in this order they shall be asked for their counsel.[40] At this point comes the only direct mention of a meal in the *Manual of Discipline* (1QS 6:4–5):[41]

והיה כיא יערוכו השולחן לאכול או התירוש לשתות, הכוהן ישלח ידו
לרשונה להברך בראשית הלחם או התירוש.

---

[35] Licht (מגילת הסרכים, 139) notes that the scribe first began to write לה, erased it, and wrote ויחד.

[36] Note that according to Philo and Josephus, the Essenes ate communal meals twice daily. See J. van der Ploeg, "The Meals of the Essenes," *JSS* 2 (1957) 167–8. According to the texts now available, the Dead Sea communal meals do not include silence or require special clothing as do the Essene meals. The requirement of ritual purity, however, is common to both the Essenes of Philo and Josephus and to the sect of Qumran. See ibid., 168–9.

[37] See L. H. Schiffman, "The Dead Sea Scrolls and the Early History of Jewish Liturgy," *The Synagogue in Late Antiquity* (ed. L. I. Levine; Philadelphia: American Schools of Oriental Research, 1987) 33–48 and idem., *Sectarian Law in the Dead Sea Scrolls, Courts, Testimony and the Penal Code* (Chico: Scholars Press, 1983) 143–4 and 153, nn. 121–23.

[38] Licht, מגילת הסרכים, 139.

[39] For a thorough analysis, see Schiffman, *Halakhah at Qumran*, 68–75.

[40] On this passage, see Schiffman, *Halakhah at Qumran*, 71.

[41] We omit the dittography in this passage with the various editors. For commentary, see the notes of Licht, מגילת הסרכים, 139 and Wernberg-Møller, *Manual*, 103, n. 17. Cf. also H. Ringgren, *The Faith of Qumran* (Philadelphia: Fortress Press, 1963) 217–20.

Whenever[42] they arrange[43] the table[44] to eat or the wine[45] to drink,[46] the priest shall extend his hand[47] first[48] to bless[49] the first[50] (portion) of the bread[51] or the wine.[52]

Several details may be noted. First, the passage indicates no obligation that all meals be communal. Second, the priest receives this honored status because of his position. The Qumranites gave special status to the Zadokite priests among them.[53] Third, bread and wine are mentioned because they were the usual food and drink. Bread was the staple food represented in many literary materials.[54] Wine was a weak, diluted, and often unfermented grape wine, similar to modern grape juice. According to the reading of 1QS this passage does not refer to a meal at which both bread and wine are required, but rather to an occasion at which the table is set for bread *or* wine. What these occasions were is not specified.

[42] On this form of כי, see Schiffman, *Sectarian Law*, 107, n. 65.

[43] Pausal form in medial position. Cf. Licht, מגילת הסרכים, 46, and E. Qimron, *The Hebrew of the Dead Sea Scrolls* (Harvard Semitic Studies 29; Altanta: Scholars Press, 1986) secs. 311. 13–14 (pp. 50–54).

[44] Cf. Isa 65:11, Prov 9:2 (Licht, מגילת הסרכים, 140). Note the mention of wine in the latter passage and the implicit allusion to it in the former. The space in the middle of השולחן in 1QS is the result of an imperfection in the parchment (ibid., 139).

[45] Licht cites *y. Ned.* 7:1 (40b bottom), which discusses the definition of תירוש. The text states that תירוש in biblical Hebrew meant wine, while it implies that it means grape juice (unfermented) in rabbinic Hebrew. Licht assumes that the text of 1QS is in biblical Hebrew and understands תירוש here as wine (מגילת הסרכים, 140).

[46] That this root refers simply to drinking, and has no banqueting connotation, is shown in Schiffman, *Sectarian Law*, 163.

[47] Perhaps "hands," assuming a defective spelling. For such spellings, see Qimron, *Hebrew*, sec. 322.141 (p. 59) and Licht, מגילת הסרכים, 47–48. Cf. *t. Ber.* 5:7 according to *ed. princ.* and parallels cited by S. Lieberman (תוספתא כפשוטה [New York: Jewish Theological Seminary, 1955] 1. 77) in which פושט ידו is used in the same sense of taking food.

[48] Phonetic spelling. Cf. Licht, מגילת הסרכים, 47 and Qimron, *Hebrew*, sec. 100.61 (pp. 22–23) and above, p. 53, in 1QSa 2:18.

[49] הפעיל used in this meaning is unattested (Licht, מגילת הסרכים, 140). Much less likely is the assumption that this is a נפעל which would require the translation, "to be blessed with. . . ."

[50] Cf. n. 23.

[51] The translation "food" would obscure the fact that the benediction over bread, as the staple of the diet, was always recited at the beginning of meals according to Jewish practice. This blessing covered all other foods.

[52] 1QS continues with a repetition of the last clause, לשתות הכוהן . . . והתירוש. The note of J. T. Milik ("The Manual of Discipline by P. Wernberg-Møller" [review], *RB* 67 [1960] 413) on the reading of ms d is ambiguous, hence the confusion between P. Guilbert ("Le plan de la 'Règle de la Communauté,'" *RQ* 1 [1958–59] 323–44) and Licht (מגילת הסרכים, 139).

[53] Cf. Schiffman, *Halakhah at Qumran*, 71–75.

[54] Licht to 1QS 6:4–6 (מגילת הסרכים, 139–40).

The Non-Sacral Nature of the Communal Meals

Dominant scholarly opinion has tended to see the communal meals of the Dead Sea sect, on analogy with the Christian eucharist, as sacral in character. This view is summarized well by B. Gärtner. He sees the sacral meal of bread and wine as central to the Qumran fellowship, tracing its origins to the temple and priestly traditions regarding the eating of sacrifices. Parallels may also be drawn, he notes, between the bread of the presence (לחם הפנים) and the Qumran "sacral meal." He goes so far as to suggest, following M. Black, that the meeting hall of the Qumran "monastery" "may have contained a table reminiscent of that on which the 'bread of Presence' was exhibited in the Temple." In this connection he also states that only those ritually pure could partake of the meals in the "Meeting hall." He correctly notes that not all of the meals of the community were eaten in this fashion. Nonetheless, he sees "The community's sacral meal" as being "an anticipation of the perfected ritual of the heavenly temple." Parallels from the meals of the Therapeutae and the Essenes as described by Philo and Josephus, respectively, are seen likewise to point "to the temple as the place of origin of their cultic meal."

Gärtner interprets in this context the purification rituals that, he claims, are in evidence in the water supply provided at one end of the "Meeting hall." Finally, he concludes:

> The Qumran sacral meal may have been intended to replace the custom of the temple priests' eating the flesh of the sacrificial animals: the holy oblation must be eaten by the sanctified in a consecrated room — a situation emphasized by the rites of purification in connection with the meal. These rites may also have included the taking of a ritual bath, a condition likewise imposed on the temple priests.[55]

Additional support for the view that the Qumran communal meal was sacral in character has been derived from comparison with the meals of the Therapeutae.[56] Although this group, according to the description of Philo, is indeed in many ways similar to the Essenes as described in Philo and Josephus as well as to the sect whose literature was found at Qumran, there are also many differences.[57]

---

[55] B. Gärtner, *The Temple and the Community in Qumran and the New Testament* (Cambridge: Cambridge University Press, 1965) 10–13. M. Delcor argues that the meals of the sect substituted for the cult and were seen by the sectarians as cultic acts ("Repas cultuels Esséniens et Thérapeutes, Thiases et Haburoth," *RQ* 6 [1967] 401–425). He bases his view on his interpretation of texts from Josephus' description of the Essenes and thereby confuses the issue.

[56] Gärtner, *Temple*, 11–12.

[57] E. Schürer, *The History of the Jewish People in the Age of Jesus Christ* (ed. G. Vermes and F. Millar; Edinburgh: T. & T. Clark, 1979) 2. 593–97. J. M. Baumgarten suggests a calendric parallel between the Therapeutae and the Qumran community ("4Q Halakha^a 5, the Law of

B. M. Bokser puts forward the argument that Philo's account of the meals of the Therapeutae was conditioned by his "religio-sociological situation as well as his philosophical stance." In particular, the meals of the Therapeutae are seen as embodying characteristics which result from the "non-Jerusalem" setting.[58] In other words, the meals of the Therapeutae, according to Bokser, served as a replacement for the temple cult in which the Therapeutae did not participate. While Bokser does not discuss the reason for their nonparticipation, it can be presumed that it resulted from distance, as there is no evidence that the Therapeutae objected to the practices of the Jerusalem priesthood, as did the authors of the Dead Sea Scrolls.

It is true that Philo's Therapeutae did celebrate their meals as a substitute for the Jerusalem cult. Yet this fact cannot be taken as evidence for the same phenomenon in the Qumran sect. Whereas the Therapeutae saw their meals as a substitute for the sacrificial service, it will be shown that no such point of view can be found in Qumran literature.

Yadin has supported the claim that the communal meals at Qumran served as substitutes for the sacrifices in which the community did not participate by citing 1QM 2:5–6. There, in a sacrificial context, occur the words ערך, "to set out," and שולחן, "table," used in the sense of "altar." These terms, as Yadin notes, also occur in the description of the communal meals at Qumran.[59] These linguistic parallels, however, do not prove Yadin's view. The use of eating and meal terminology in relation to sacrifices results from the concept found in the Bible and throughout the ancient Near East that sacrifices are a sort of meal, for or with the god(s).[60] Hence, the cultic use of these terms. A glance at the lexica will reveal that these same usages are common in the Bible, and no one would maintain that there took place communal meals as a substitute for the temple cult in biblical times.

J. van der Ploeg has defined the sacral meal and discussed it in detail:[61]

> Since the essential act of a meal is the eating of the food, a meal can only
> be called sacred when the eating is a sacred act. This is normally the case

---

Hadash, and the Pentacontad Calendar," *JJS* 27 [1976] 39–41). Some differences regarding the meals are as follows: the Therapeutae did not serve wine or grape juice, but water (Philo *Contemplative Life* 73). They prohibited the drinking of wine (74) or eating of meat (73). The Scriptural study practiced by the Therapeutae (76–78) was not part of the Qumran meal, nor were the hymns (80). There is no mention of grace in the account of the Therapeutae. On the meals of the Essenes, see Josephus, *J.W.* 2.8.5. §129–33.

[58] B. M. Bokser, "Philo's Description of Jewish Practices," *Protocol of the Thirtieth Colloquy: 5 June 1977* (Berkeley: Center for Hermeneutical Studies, 1977) 1–11. See also his *The Origin of the Seder* (Berkeley, Los Angeles and London: University of California Press, 1984) 56–62.

[59] Yadin, *War Scroll*, 200.

[60] This theme is discussed repeatedly in W. R. Smith, *The Religion of the Semites* (New York: Schocken, 1972). Although the lectures making up this book were delivered in 1888–91, this observation remains valid.

[61] Van der Ploeg, "The Meals of the Essenes," 164–66. The quotation is on 165.

when the food is sacred or when a sacred meaning is attached to it. In an article in the encyclopaedia, *Die Religion in Geschichte und Gegenwart* (2nd ed.),[62] F. Pfister knows of four kinds of "cultic meals" (*kultische Mahl-zeiten*): meals in which holy food is eaten; covenant meals; the meal of the sacrifice of communion; the meal offered exclusively to a god.

There simply is no evidence that the "meal" described in the Qumran passage cited above is a cultic or sacred meal. The purity of food and drink and the rituals associated with grace before and after meals were certainly widespread by this time, and in no way can it be said that every meal was sacral. All the motifs — purity, benedictions, bread and wine, and the role of the priest — can be explained against the background of contemporary Jewish ceremonial and ritual practice.[63]

First and foremost among the so-called "sacral" ingredients in this meal is the aspect of the role of the priest.[64] It should therefore be explained that a tannaitic tradition of the House of Rabbi Ishmael lists privileges of this nature granted to the priests in recognition of their cultic status. The ברייתא, basing itself on Lev 21:8, states[65] that a priest should be given the opportunity to be called to read the first portion of the Torah[66] (which includes the recitation of the initial benediction), to pronounce the grace after meals first,[67] and to receive first the best portion of

---

[62] F. Pfister, *RGG* (1929) 3. 854–55.

[63] Note van der Ploeg's conclusion, "that the writings of Philo and Josephus . . . do not give us sufficient arguments to say that the Essenes had sacred meals. They only speak of the common, communal meals, and it would have been an exception to the rule observed everywhere, that true meals are only sacred in certain circumstances" ("The Meals of the Essenes," 171). A similar view is espoused by Smith, "God's Begetting the Messiah," 219.

[64] For the role of the priest in the Hellenistic cultic banquets (thiases), cf. Delcor, "Repas," 410–12.

[65] *B. Git.* 59b; *b. Ned.* 62a–b; *b. Hor.* 12b; *b. Mo'ed Qat.* 28b. The ברייתא, according to its attribution, should be dated to the latter half of the second century CE. Tosafot to *b. Hul.* 87a asserts that Lev 21:8 serves here only as an אסמכתא, meaning that the precedence of the priest is only a rabbinical ordinance. On the other hand, Abraham Abele ben Hayyim Ha-Levi Gombiner (מגן אברהם, to שולחן ערוך, אורח חיים 201, paragraph 4) says that it is a biblical ordinance (דאורייתא) and notes that it appears in Maimonides' ספר המצות (עשה no. 32 [ed. H. Heller; Jerusalem: Mossad Harav Kook, 1979/80] 45).

[66] So pseudo-Rashi to *b. Mo'ed Qat.* 28b; pseudo-Rashi and Ran to *b. Ned.* 62b; and pseudo-Rashi to *b. Hor.* 12b. Rashi to *b. Git.* 59b, however, takes לפתוח ראשון in a wider sense and sees it as indicating that the priest should take precedence in regard to any honor. Whether it is the reading of the Torah or the study session (ישיבה), he should be called upon first. Cf. the statement of the amora Rabbi Joshua ben Levi in *y. Ber.* 5:4 (5:5, 9d) and *y. Git.* 5:9 (47b) the context of which shows that it refers to the priest's precedence in the reading of the Torah.

[67] Hebrew ולברך ראשון. So pseudo-Rashi to *b. Mo'ed Qat.* 28b. Pseudo-Rashi to *b. Hor.* 12b understands this as referring to recitation of the זימון, the invitation to say grace after meals, recited when at least three males have eaten together. Pseudo-Rashi to *b. Ned.* 62a, however, sees the reference here as being to the grace both before and after the meal, giving precedence to the priest in both.

food.[68] These procedures were probably ancient customs which showed no more than the deep reverence in which priest, temple, and cult were held by the people. The demonstration of this respect in no way transformed the meal into a sacral occasion. On the contrary, if the meal were a sacral occasion, the privileges of the priest would be confined to areas in which *only* he might function. Rather, he is simply granted the opportunity to perform first rituals which each and every Jew present may fulfill.

The second motif usually seen as "sacral" is ritual purity. There is, of course, no question that the members of the sect ate their communal meals in a state of ritual purity. This concern is reflected in the process by which a person might enter the sect. 1QS 6:13–23 contains prescriptions regarding the entrance of new members. These regulations, which we have elsewhere discussed in detail,[69] explain how the new recruit is progressively brought closer to complete membership. Part of this process relates to his coming into contact with the food and drink of the community. He is first allowed contact, after more than a year, with the pure solid food of the community (טהרת הרבים). After a second year he is allowed contact with the liquid food (משקה הרבים). This distinction between liquid and solid foods is similar to that of the tannaitic sources. Because liquids render foods susceptible to impurity, the regulations regarding drink are stricter.

These purity laws, however, should not be confused with sacred meals. First, the laws of purity were to be observed by members at all times, whether they ate alone or communally. After all, these laws were the ancient heritage of the priesthood, and the Qumran sect, like the Pharisees, extended them to a wider range of initiates. Second, purity of food was an obligation which did not impart any sacral character to the act of eating. One might say that these purity laws were, from a functional point of view, similar to the laws of כשרות, although it must be emphasized that according to Jewish law they are two distinct entities.

Nor do the benedictions recited by the priest render the meal sacral. The tannaitic tradition mentioned above has been variously interpreted to indicate that the priest was entitled to the honor of reciting grace before and after the meal before the other participants.[70] In fact, such benedictions are a regular part of tannaitic tradition and are meant to emphasize man's dependence on the Creator for daily sustenance.[71] By early tannaitic times, blessings both before and after meals were most probably part of the life of the חבורה. Indeed, the so-called סדר הסעודה, the order of the procedure

---

[68] So Rashi to *b. Git.* 59b, and Ran to *b. Ned.* 62b. (Pseudo-Rashi's interpretation of *b. Ned.* 62b would make sense only if the ברייתא applied to the high priest.) Among the examples of the application of this principle, Tosafot to *b. Git.* 59b, *s.v.* וליטול, mentions חברים eating a meal (סעודה) together.

[69] Schiffman, *Sectarian Law*, 161–65.

[70] See above, nn. 66–67.

[71] *T. Ber.* 4:1.

for the formal dinner embedded in the Tosefta,[72] is probably a reflection of the common dining patterns of Greco-Roman Palestine[73] somewhat refined by the tannaitic tradition. While there is no actual proof, it is extremely tempting to say that such procedures would have been followed by the members of the חבורת, at least in the last years of the Second Temple period.[74]

In the tannaitic traditions such benedictions were part of all meals, whether formal or informal.[75] In fact, they had to be recited for anything eaten, and they bear no sacral connotations. In the same spirit are to be understood the benedictions mentioned in Josephus' description of the Essenes. There the priest says grace before and after the meal.[76] Josephus correctly interprets this practice in light of Palestinian Jewish custom of his day when he says that "at the beginning and at the close they do homage to God as the bountiful giver of life."[77]

Here again the non-sacral, i.e. non-sacrificial, aspect of this grace must be emphasized. Indeed, despite the many assertions to the contrary, the entire description of the meal of the Essenes contains no sacral elements. Nowhere is it stated or even hinted that this meal was a replacement for the sacrificial cult. On the contrary, the rules of purity and benedictions followed in it had a character and importance of their own. By this time they were totally divorced from the temple context and part of the daily life of many pious Palestinian Jews of the time, whether Essenes, Pharisees, or members of the group whose texts were deposited at Qumran.

The passages before us refer to the eating of bread and the drinking of wine. The order in which these foods appear has caused some difficulty to scholars seeking to draw parallels with the rabbinic tradition. Because of the prominence of the קדוש ("sanctification") prayer said over wine before the Sabbath evening[78] and morning[79] meals, questions have been raised regarding the order of the menu in our passage in which the bread precedes the wine. No such problem need be raised. The tannaitic passages regarding the

---

[72] *T. Ber.* 4:8. Note the lengthy advice on eating and drinking in Ben Sira 31:12–32:13.

[73] So Lieberman, תוספתא כפשוטה, 1. 62–63.

[74] J. M. Baumgarten notes that there is no evidence that the חבורה had communal meals ("Qumran Studies," *JBL* 77 [1958] 251).

[75] *M. Ber.* 6–7. Grace before meals is presumed in Matt 14:19.

[76] Thackeray's translation of τροφῆς as "meat" is too narrow. A better translation would be "food" or "meal" (cf. Liddell and Scott, 1827).

[77] *J.W.* 2.7.5 §131 (LCL, trans. Thackeray).

[78] The evening "sanctification" prayer is already presumed in a dispute of the House of Hillel and the House of Shammai recorded in *m. Ber.* 8:1.

[79] *Mekhilta' De-Rabbi Ishmael, Yitro* 7 (ed. H. S. Horovitz and I. A. Rabin; Jerusalem: Bamberger and Wahrmann, 1960, p. 229); *Mekhilta' De-Rabbi Shimʿon ben Yohai* to Exod 20:8 (ed. J. N. Epstein and E. Z. Melammed; Jerusalem: Mekize Nirdamin, 1955, p. 149); בריתא and amoraic discussion in *b. Pesaḥ.* 106a.

procedure for the formal dinner, apparently concerning dinners not held on the Sabbath, describe as normal procedure the drinking of wine which was served during the meal. Such wine was brought to the table after the grace before meals had been said and the accompanying bread had been eaten.[80] This was no doubt the case in our text. The bread is that over which the grace before meals is said.[81] The wine is the wine served during the meal, not that used for the קדוש on Sabbath and festivals.

In the messianic banquet the benedictions on the bread are recited by the priest and the messiah of Israel. Then each of the other guests, the members of the sect, recites his own benediction. Licht correctly notes that this procedure is in direct opposition to the pattern found in early tannaitic texts describing formal meals at which the grace is recited by one, thereby fulfilling the obligation of all.[82]

In any case, it must be reemphasized that the recitation of benedictions before the meal and at its conclusion by a priest and the required ritual purity at the meal in no way rendered the meal sacral. Rather these traditions were part of everyday life for the Jews of Palestine by this time and were observed by all "sects" at every formal dinner or banquet regardless of its context. It can be expected that meals of groups, including family celebrations, the Passover Seder, and the meals of the Sabbaths and festivals, all followed these patterns in the Hasmonean and Herodian periods.

Archaeological Evidence of the Communal Meal

For the Dead Sea group we are fortunate in having not only the written remains in the form of the scrolls, but also the archaeological materials which shed so much light on life at Qumran. Archaeologists have established beyond a doubt that those who hid the scrolls in the caves are the same as those who inhabited the ruins at Qumran. It can, therefore, be established that here existed facilities for communal meals, and that remains of such meals may be found, whereas there is no evidence for a sacrificial cult.

Already during period Ib of Qumran's occupation, extending approximately from the reign of John Hyrcanus (135–104 BCE)[83] until the

---

[80] M. Ber. 6:6; t. Ber. 4:8 (סדר הסעודה), 10.

[81] Loaves were specifically provided for that purpose in the Essene meal. See Josephus J.W. 2.8.5 §130.

[82] Licht, מגילת הסרכים, 140, 270. For grace before meals, see m. Ber. 6:6 that specifically states that in informal meals (at which the guests sit) the grace before meals is recited individually, whereas at formal meals (at which the guests recline) the grace before meals is recited by one on behalf of all. According to Tosafot to b. Ber. 42a this משנה applies as well to grace after meals.

[83] R. de Vaux, Archaeology and the Dead Sea Scrolls (London: Oxford University Press, 1973) 19. E. M. Laperrousaz, Qoumrân, l'établissement Essénien des bords de la Mer Morte (Paris: A. & J. Picard, 1976) 29–33 has discussed in detail de Vaux's dating of the end of period Ia and

earthquake of 31 BCE,[84] the largest room of the Qumran buildings was a hall 22m. long and 4.5m. wide. The existence of a system for washing and draining the floor of this room has led scholars to the conclusion that it served as a dining facility and was used for the eating of communal meals. In an adjoining room were found some one thousand pottery vessels. These had been stacked according to type.[85] R. de Vaux has concluded that this was a storage room for the vessels used in the dining room.[86]

In addition, one kitchen with several fireplaces was unearthed.[87] The kitchen, pottery storeroom, and dining hall continued in use during period II,[88] that, according to de Vaux, lasted from the outset of the reign of Herod Archelaus (between 4 and 1 BCE)[89] to the Great Revolt against Rome. R. de Vaux has taken the view that Qumran was destroyed in June of 68 CE by the Romans.[90] He estimates that the group using these facilities "would not have numbered many more than two hundred members."[91]

Connected with the problem of meals at Qumran is the finding (primarily from period Ib) of deposits of animal bones buried between or around the buildings, placed in large sherds of pitchers or pots or in intact jars with their lids on.[92] These deposits are usually flush with the ground level. Examination

the beginning of period Ib. He shows that de Vaux has vacillated through the years as to the exact dates and criticizes his evaluation of the numismatic evidence. Laperrousaz concludes (33) that it is impossible on archaeological grounds precisely to place period Ia within the last century of the Hellenistic period of Palestine. By this he means (cf. 33, n. 2) that period Ia might be fixed anywhere from 163–63 BCE. Hence, he is unable to suggest an exact date within the Hasmonean period for the onset of period Ib (38).

[84] De Vaux, *Archaeology*, 20–21. Laperrousaz, basing himself on detailed numismatic study, would date the end of period Ib to between 67 and 63 BCE. It is quite clear from the discussion (Laperrousaz, *Qoumrân*, 38–45) that the evidence is susceptible to various interpretations. There can be no question, however, that this period ceased at least by the earthquake of 31 BCE.

[85] See de Vaux, *Archaeology*, plates Xa and Xb.

[86] De Vaux, *Archaeology*, 11–12. Laperrousaz (*Qoumrân*, 35–36) notes that the pottery in question has been attributed to period II by J. T. Milik on the basis of paleographic evidence.

[87] De Vaux, *Archaeology*, 7, 10.

[88] Laperrousaz, *Qoumrân*, 47.

[89] Laperrousaz fixes the beginning of period IIa during the reign of Herod the Great (37–4 BCE). He suggests a second abandonment of the site which would, according to him, have resulted probably from the transformation of Judea into a procuratorial province in 6 CE (*Qoumrân*, 50–56). This second abandonment is purely hypothetical and rests on insufficient evidence.

[90] De Vaux, *Archaeology*, 33–41, followed by Laperrousaz, *Qoumrân*, 56–58.

[91] De Vaux, *Archaeology*, 86. Laperrousaz makes a detailed study of this question (ibid., 99–109). He concludes that 300–350 people would have lived at Qumran during period Ib, and perhaps 350–400 would have occupied Qumran and Ein Feshka during periods IIa and IIb of Qumran (109). De Vaux's figure is not far removed from those of Milik (150–200) and Farmer ("a few hundred regular members") (de Vaux, *Archaeology*, 86, n. 1). We must also bear in mind that Laperrousaz is the first to take so seriously the facilities at Ein Feshka, as evidenced by his devoting pp. 63–90 of his study to this site.

[92] See de Vaux, *Archaeology*, plates XIa and XIb.

of the bones shows that no deposit contained an entire skeleton. The bones had been taken apart and the flesh removed before burial. Many contain bones of a single type of animal, and the remainder represent two, three, or four types. Animals included are: adult sheep, adult goats, lambs or kids, calves, cows, or oxen.[93] Many scholars have sought to explain these bones as either the remains of sacrifices or sacral meals. Without question they are bones of animals used for food. It has been determined that the meat was generally boiled and less often roasted. R. de Vaux states that the careful burials indicate a "religious preoccupation."[94] He is hesitant to conclude that these animals are the remains of sacrificial rites. First, he says, no altar or cult place has been found at Qumran.[95] Second, we may add, the texts from Qumran make plain the community's view regarding sacrifice. They abstained from temple offerings because of what they saw as the impurity of the cult as it was conducted by the Jerusalem establishment.[96] In the messianic era the Qumranites would return victoriously to the "New Jerusalem" where they would reconstitute the cult according to their views and with their own priestly messiah at its head.[97] There is no room in such a schema for sacrifice at Qumran.[98]

Numerous attempts have been made to explain the reason for the burial of these bones.[99] None of these is satisfactory inasmuch as there is no literary

---

[93] For detailed accounts of the finds, see Laperrousaz, *Qoumrân*, 215–18 and J.-L. Duhaime, "Remarques sur les dépôts d'ossements d'animaux à Qumrân," *RQ* 9 (1977) 245–47.

[94] De Vaux, *Archaeology*, 14.

[95] Ibid., 12–14.

[96] See J. M. Baumgarten, "Sacrifice and Worship among the Jewish Sectarians of the Dead Sea (Qumran) Scrolls," *HTR* 46 (1953) 141–57; Schiffman, *Halakhah at Qumran*, 78; Cross, *Ancient Library*, 101–3; L. Ginzberg, *An Unknown Jewish Sect* (New York: Jewish Theological Seminary, 1971) 117, 281, 384–86; van der Ploeg, "The Meals of the Essenes," 172; and J. Nolland, "A Misleading Statement of the Essene Attitude to the Temple," *RQ* 9 (1977–78) 555–62.

[97] The "New Jerusalem" is the theme of several Aramaic texts from Qumran on which see DJD 1. 134–35; 3. 84–89, 184–93. Cultic ceremonies would form part of the final battle described in the *War Scroll*. For a thorough analysis, see Yadin, *War Scroll*, 198–228. On the *Temple Scroll*, see Schiffman, *Sectarian Law*, 13–14.

[98] Cross reaches the opposite conclusion, though with some hesitation (*Ancient Library*, 102). He bases his opinion on the animal bones, but does not deal with the objections raised here. J. van der Ploeg discusses the attitude to sacrifice of the Essenes of Philo and Josephus ("The Meals of the Essenes," 170). He takes the view that while the Essenes did not sacrifice in the temple, they replaced the sacrificial cult with nonsacrificial ceremonies of their own. See also J. Bowman, "Did the Qumran Sect Burn the Red Heifer?" *RQ* 1 (1958) 73–84 and G. Klinzing, *Die Umdeutung des Kultus in der Qumrangemeinde und im Neuen Testament* (Göttingen: Vandenhoeck & Ruprecht, 1971) 20–49.

[99] A thorough survey is given in de Vaux, *Archaeology*, 14–16, n. 3. See also Laperrousaz, *Qoumrân*, 211–15; Duhaime, "Remarques," 249–51; and E. M. Laperrousaz, "A propos des dépôts d'ossements d'animaux trouvés à Qoumrân," *RQ* (1978) 569–73. Cf. also J. M. Baumgarten, "The Pharisaic-Sadducean Controversies about Purity and the Qumran Texts," *JJS* 31 (1980) 161–64.

evidence for the burial of bones in any Jewish sacrificial or religious rite.[100] Further, the archaeological parallels which have been cited are of questionable relevance. While it is possible that these bones are the remains of communal meals, their burial in the dining hall cannot be explained. There is no choice but to admit that until further discoveries, no satisfactory explanation can be offered. At all events, archaeological evidence shows that the facilities for communal meals were present at Qumran and that for some reason the remains of these meals were buried around the dining room.

These meals, conducted regularly as part of the present-age way of life of the sect, were preenactments of the final messianic banquet which the sectarians expected in the soon-to-come end of days. Again, the life of the sect in this world mirrored its dreams for the age to come.

[100] The *Temple Scroll* contains no reference to this or any similar practice among detailed prescriptions for the sacrificial offerings.

5

CONCLUSION: THE ESCHATON
AS A MIRROR OF THE PRESENT

The Dead Sea Sect expected that the end of days would inaugurate an era of perfection in which they would see the culmination of the rituals and regulations practiced in the present, pre-messianic age. The eschatological community would be structured as a reflection of the present community. Members would progress through the stages of life demarcated by their ages and responsibilities and the degree of their initiation into sectarian life. Those of sufficient stature, who attained the highest standards of ritual purity, would participate in the holy convocations of the community. However, those who, due to various physical defects, would have been disqualified from priestly service would be denied entry into the assemblies of the group. These assemblies would conduct the affairs of the sect, pass judgment, and declare war. As in the period of the desert wandering, the Levites would assume defined leadership roles in the future life of the sect. It was the Zadokite priesthood, however, which was expected to be the dominant force in the end of days.

When the messianic war begins, the sect will be mustered to fight the battles against the evildoers and those who do not know the correct interpretation of the Torah which the sect expounds. As the sect finally overcomes its enemies and is seen to be victorious, the righteous of Israel who turn to God and adopt the sectarian way of life will also be included in the sect. Together with the original sectarians, they will constitute the eschatological community.

This new community will gather together for the messianic banquet presumably in the aftermath of the great War between the Sons of Light and the Sons of Darkness. Under the leadership of the Zadokite priestly messiah and the messiah of Israel, they will reconstitute the life of Israel on its land in accord with the views of the sect. Together the people of Israel will live the life of purity and perfection.

The description of the eschatological congregation in the *Rule of the Congregation* repeatedly mirrors the regulations of the sect for the present age found in other Qumran texts. Further, since the congregation of the end of days would fight the great final battle described in the *War Scroll*, many of the prescriptions of this scroll were found to coincide with the regulations of the *Rule of the Congregation*. The coincidence of legislation and procedure for the present age, the eschatological battle, and the end of days also demonstrates that the sect attempted in the present age to actualize its dreams for the better days to come, and, therefore, to anticipate the perfect holiness which it believed would typify that coming age. For this reason, the list of ages in the *Rule of the Congregation* conforms almost completely to the norms governing the ages of the sectarian officials and to the ages of the military units of the final battle.

Further, the sect saw itself as embodying the role of its leadership, the Zadokite priesthood. It even referred to itself as the Sons of Zadok, and accented over and over again the leadership and decision-making role of this group of priests. Even if this role had, as argued by some, become virtually ceremonial by the later period of the sect's history, it was still ingrained in the sect's self-image. Hence, the sectarians expected this role to continue in the end of days. In this way we can understand that consistently the source for the age limits found in our text—whether for present-day officials of the sect, military stations in the eschatological battle, or the structure of the messianic community—is the Levitical legislation of the Pentateuch. The sect appropriated these age requirements and used them to derive the stages of sectarian responsibility.

We can see here, as in the *Zadokite Fragments*, that there is no reason to believe that the sect was celibate. Sexual relations are to be permitted in the eschatological community. From the *Zadokite Fragments* we know that they were permitted to members of the sect in the sectarian settlements. Certainly, the growth and education of children is assumed in both texts as well as in the *War Scroll*. These must have been children of members of the sect who would one day take their place in the community, both in the present and in the end of days. We learn from our text of the thorough educational system for young children which must have existed at Qumran as it would exist in the end of days.

The Dead Sea sect, in seeking to achieve the highest standards of purity and perfection in the end of days, maintained the exclusion of certain classes of those afflicted with impurity, physical deformities or old age from the eschatological assembly. These prohibitions were derived from Leviticus 13 and 21, passages regarding the disqualification of priests from temple service. After all, the sect saw itself as constituting a sanctuary through its dedication to a life of holiness and purity. It therefore extended the Torah's legislation regarding the priesthood to its eschatological assembly.

It is most probable that the very same regulations were in force in the present age, in which the sect lived in preparation for and in expectation of the dawn of the *eschaton*. Indeed, the sect expected that very similar regulations would be in effect regarding the camp in the eschatological battle. The eschatological council described in the *Rule of the Congregation* would represent what the Qumran sect believed was the highest standard of purity and perfection. Only in this way could the sectarians, together with the holy angels, live the life of the future age.

As a reflection of the deep messianic consciousness of this group, participation in the communal meals was a central eschatological ritual. The messianic banquets to be presided over by the priest and the messiah of Israel were enacted as well in the day-to-day lives of the sectarians at their communal meals. They saw these meals as a foretaste of the world to come. Both the messianic meals and those of this world required a quorum of ten, ritual purity of the participants, bread and wine, or either of them. The priest is accorded the honor of blessing the food before anyone else is allowed to partake of it. The members of the congregation sit in order of their status, and in this order they bless the food.

Despite the ritual purity required to participate in the meals and the role of the priest, this type of meal cannot be considered a sacral meal. The procedures here described were not replacements for the cultic sacrifices of the Jerusalem temple. Rather, they were already part of the rituals of the Jews of Palestine during this period.

In looking forward to the messianic era, the sect utilized the terminology of the Exodus from Egypt and the desert-wandering period in Israelite history. This period served as the prototype of the ultimate redemption, for it represented the closest possible relationship to God, with God's direct intervention in history and His revelation of the law. At that time, too, Israel had been faithful to the correct teachings. The sectarian expected the renewal of this ancient grandeur in the soon to dawn *eschaton*. So it is not surprising that this biblical terminology and, specifically, the terminology of the military encampment and organization of the desert-period is everywhere in evidence in our text.

The author of our text looked to the end of days for the restoration of the ancient glories of Israel. The monarchy, the true high priesthood, the tribal organization, all these were to be relived in the end of days. At the same time, he looked forward to a level of sanctity and purity impossible in the present age. To him, the perfect observance of the law of the Torah represented the ideal. In his vision, as in the Qumran sect's eschatology as a whole, the restorative and utopian trends of Jewish messianism played an equal role. The coming cataclysm would inaugurate both a return to the past and a new and previously unachievable future of observance of the law, ritual purity and perfection. It is this combination of trends which made possible the messianic fervor and immediacy which characterized the Dead Sea sect.

Our text represents the way in which the ancient, formative history of Israel in the desert-period, the present pre-messianic age, and the great battle and assembly to come, are seen by the sectarian as reflections one of the other. The redemption from Egypt and the desert-wandering, crowned by the revelation at Sinai, were for the sectarian a paradigm of that which would be once again repeated in the end of days in which he was soon to share. He himself would experience the great battles and tribulations. For the present, however, he would strive to live in the perfect holiness of the future age. As a result, he would eventually merit the experience of the revelation of God's glory in the end of days, a promise he felt certain would be fulfilled in his lifetime.

APPENDIX:

THE RULE OF BENEDICTIONS AND ITS PLACE IN THE RULE SCROLL

The Reconstruction of the Text

The text of the *Rule of Benedictions* (סרך הברכות) contains a series of blessings which the משכיל, a term to be returned to below, is to recite. Each of the benedictions is preceded by a prose introduction which specifies who is to be blessed. The text is extremely fragmentary, yet three such introductions can be distinguished, directed to the יראי אל[, "those who fear God," the בני צדוק הכוהנים, "the Zadokite priests," and the נשיא העדה, "the Prince of the congregation." Beyond this, the fragmentary nature of the text has led scholars to posit various reconstructions according to which the opening rubrics of additional blessings are assumed to have stood in what are now the lacunae.

J. T. Milik, in the *editio princeps*,[1] suggested the following reconstruction:

1:1–20   Blessing of the Faithful (יראי אל)
1:21–3:20 Blessing of the High Priest
3:21–5:19 Blessing of the Priests
5:20–29   Blessing of the Prince (נשיא) of the Congregation

This schema has been challenged by J. Licht.[2] Licht begins with the assumption that this text is intended to be recited at a public ceremony at the end of days. Further, he suggests that the text must have included blessings for the various ranks within the congregation of the end of days that are mentioned in the *Rule of the Congregation*. The fragmentary nature of the *Rule of Benedictions* does not allow us to identify all of them. Licht suggests that the text begins with the יראי אל, who are the lowest (we have shown this to be a term for the members of the sect),[3] and proceeds to the blessing of the most important eschatological figures of the sect, the High Priest and

[1] J. T. Milik in D. Barthélemy and J. T. Milik, *Qumran Cave I*, Discoveries in the Judaean Desert 1 (Oxford: Clarendon Press, 1955) 118–130.

[2] J. Licht, מגילת הסרכים (Jerusalem: Mosad Bialik, 1965) 274–75.

[3] L. H. Schiffman, *Sectarian Law in the Dead Sea Scrolls, Courts, Testimony and the Penal Code* (Chico: Scholars Press, 1983) 60.

the Prince of the Congregation. Licht, therefore, cannot agree with Milik, who assumed that the blessing of the High Priest preceded that of the other priests. Licht sees the blessing of the High Priest as too long according to the reconstruction of Milik. For these reasons, Licht analyzes the text as follows:

1:1–9	Blessing of the Faithful (יראי אל)
2:22–28	Blessing of an Unidentified Group
3:1–6	Blessing of an Official or Group of Importance
3:17–21	Blessing of an Unidentified Group
3:22–28	Blessing of the Zadokite Priests
4:22–28	Blessing of the High Priest
5:18–19	Unidentified
5:20–29	Blessing of the Prince of the Congregation[4]

Apparently working independently of Licht, J. Carmignac also disputed the reconstruction of Milik, although less substantially.[5] He sees the first benediction as directed to the members of the community. That which occupies the top of column 3 would concern the High Priest. That which begins in 3:22 refers to the Zadokite Priests. The text which begins in 5:20 refers to the Prince of the Congregation. The rest, he says, is subject to conjecture. Like Licht, he is doubtful about Milik's long benediction for the High Priest. Carmignac asks: Where are the ordinary priests, the Levites, the notables, the officers of the army (as described in 1QSa)? Accordingly, he titles 2:1–3:21 "Other Benedictions."

While Carmignac is certainly correct that much in the reconstruction of this text is left to conjecture, there can be no question that an adequate schema would take into account the nature of the scroll as a whole, in which the *Rule of Benedictions* appears as the last part. Whereas the first text, the *Manual of Discipline,* attempts to set out the perfect community for the present, pre-messianic age, that of the *Rule of the Congregation* describes the community of the end of days and its final assembly. Licht's reconstruction of the original contents of our text has the advantage that it takes into account the description of the eschatological community outlined in the *Rule of the Congregation* as a basis for analysis. He expects to find in our text a series of benedictions for the very same officials mentioned in the *Rule of the Congregation.* His reconstruction is therefore to be preferred. Further, his detailed commentary on the material and his careful evaluation of Milik's readings and restorations, with which he for the most part agrees, argue strongly for Licht's analysis.

---

[4] Licht, מגילת הסרכים, 274–75.
[5] J. Carmignac, "Le recueil des bénédictions," *Les textes de Qumran* (ed. J. Carmignac, É. Cothenet and H. Lignée; Paris: Letouzey et Ané, 1963) 2. 31.

On the other hand, some differences in terminology between the *Rule of the Congregation* and the *Rule of Benedictions* ought to caution against automatically assuming that all those who appear in the *Rule of the Congregation* are blessed in the *Rule of Benedictions*. Indeed, it is likely that these two texts were composed by different authors. We cannot accept the conclusion of Carmignac that this work, along with the *Manual of Discipline*, the *Scroll of the War of the Sons of Light against the Sons of Darkness*, the *Hodayot Scroll*, and the *Rule of the Congregation* were all composed by the teacher of righteousness.[6]

Literary Background

It has already been noted that each blessing began with a formula stating that these words of blessing were to be recited by the משכיל in praise of the specified group. The analysis of the term משכיל in the Qumran sectarian corpus has generated a considerable literature.[7] Suffice it to say that this term is to be taken as designating not only one who is wise, but also one who instructs others in his wisdom. Such instructors, as can be seen from the parallels in Dan 11:33–34 and 12:3, prepare the way for the end of days by teaching the רבים, the Many, a term which the sect used to describe itself. At Qumran, the job of the משכיל is to teach the sectarians the beliefs and observances of the sect, especially as regards the doctrine of the two spirits and its practical ramifications. He is to exemplify the sectarian way of life (1QS 3:13–15, 9:12–26). In so doing, he prepares the way for the final age of perfection.

Licht already noted that the priestly blessing (Num 6:24–26) plays a prominent role in our text.[8] Indeed, most of the text may be regarded as an expansion upon the priestly blessing. The following list of phrases from the *Rule of Benedictions* which occur in the priestly blessing of Numbers demonstrates this dependence:

1:3	יברככה א[דני]
1:5	[וי]חו[נ]כה
2:22–27	[ו]יחונכה occurs on every line
3:1	ישא אדני פניו אליכה
3:3	פניו . . . ישא
3:4	יש[א]
3:21	שלומכה
3:25	יברככה אדני

[6] Ibid., 2. 32.

[7] For bibliography, see L. H. Schiffman, *The Halakhah at Qumran* (Leiden: E. J. Brill, 1975) 25, n. 24.

[8] Licht, מגילת הסרכים, 275–76.

At the same time, such parallels cannot be cited for the last two blessings of the text (following Licht's analysis). In view of the dependency of the benediction for the Prince of the Congregation on Isa 11:2–5, it is likely that this benediction, even in its complete form, did not take its cue from the priestly blessing. The same is probably true of the benediction for the High Priest in our text. Licht points to similarities between the benediction for the High Priest and certain parts of early versions of the 'Avodah Service for the Day of Atonement.

The Function of the Benedictions

The dependence of most of the benedictions on the priestly blessing makes possible a suggestion about the precise *Sitz im Leben* of the text under discussion. 1QS 2:2–4 also contains an adaptation of the priestly blessing to be recited as part of the blessing and curse ceremony that was an annual event in the life of the sect. This ceremony involved the full mustering of the members of the sect and their participation in a covenant renewal ceremony. The priests would recite an expanded priestly blessing for the members of the sect, אנשי גורל אל, "men of the lot of God." The Levites then recited a curse formula, in reality a reversal of the expanded priestly blessing, for the people of the גורל בליעל, "the lot of Belial" (1QS 1:16–2:18).

These two lots were to exist for all the days of the reign of Belial (ממשלת בליעל). Throughout that period, the one in which the sect saw itself as living, this annual mustering and covenant renewal were to take place (1QS 2:19–25). The mustering that is described is a detailed one, and one cannot help noticing that the principles of organization for the mustering of the sect are exactly like those of the eschatological community of the *Rule of the Congregation*. In other words, the very same kind of mustering was to take place in the end of days as occurred in the present, pre-messianic age.

In the end of days, there would no longer be a "lot of Belial" to curse. Only the sect and its followers would survive the great battles described in the *Scroll of the War of the Sons of Light against the Sons of Darkness* and the resulting destruction of the wicked. Therefore, only the blessing formula would have to be recited. The benedictions of the *Rule of Benedictions* are intended to replace the blessing and curse recited as part of the mustering and covenant renewal. The blessings preserved in our text represent the eschatological benedictions of the present age, which the sect believed would be recited at the dawn of the *eschaton,* at the mustering ceremony. Besides the benediction for the entire sect (the יראי אל), benedictions would be recited for each specific group of dignitaries.

The passage from Isaiah which served as the basis for the blessing of the Prince of the Congregation was of great significance in the eschatological thought of the sect, as can be gathered from its use in other passages. 4Q161 (Commentary on Isaiah [A]) 8–10 contains quotations of Isa 11:1–5 and a pesher-exegesis of them. The basic thrust of the exegesis can be seen in the clause, [פשרו על צמח] דויד העומד באחרית הימים]. ("[Its interpretation concerns the shoot of] David who will arise at the e[nd of days . . .].")[9] This Isaiah passage was to the sect a prophecy regarding the messiah son of David who according to some views may be identical with the Prince of the Congregation of the end of days, termed משיח ישראל in the *Rule of the Congregation*. He will rule, together with the priestly messiah who is identical with the High Priest of the *Rule of the Congregation*.

Immediately following this chapter in Isaiah comes another which was of great importance to the sect. Chapter 12 of Isaiah begins by stating that with the coming of what the sect took as the messianic deliverer, "You shall say on that day, I will give thanks to You O Lord. . . ." This passage is the only place in the Bible that the expression אודך comes at the beginning of a song and it is this notion of a messianic song of praise that must have provided the basic form for the *Thanksgiving Hymns*.

The entire *Rule of Benedictions* is a set of hymns to be recited as part of the mustering ceremony to be held in the end of days. This mustering is mentioned explicitly in *Rule of the Congregation* 1:22–25. At this mustering there would no longer be a need to recite blessings and curses, for there was no reason to utter the previously customary imprecations. At this end of days, it would only be necessary to praise the sect and its leaders, for the ultimate perfection had dawned, and they had been its harbingers.

---

[9] J. M. Allegro, *Qumrân Cave 4*, Discoveries in the Judean Desert 5 (Oxford: Clarendon Press, 1968) 14.

BIBLIOGRAPHY

Albeck, Ch. (ed.) ששה סדרי משנה. 6 vols. Jerusalem, Tel Aviv: Mosad Bialik, Dvir, 1957–59.

Allegro, J. M. *Qumrân Cave 4*. Discoveries in the Judaean Desert 5. Oxford: Clarendon Press, 1968.

Babylonian Talmud. Vilna edition (with commentaries and Alfasi). 20 vols. New York: Otzar Hasefarim, 1964.

Baillet, M. *Qumrân Grotte 4, III (4Q482–4Q520)*. Discoveries in the Judaean Desert 7. Oxford: Clarendon Press, 1982.

Baillet, M., J. T. Milik, and R. de Vaux. *Les 'Petites Grottes' de Qumrân*. Discoveries in the Judaean Desert of Jordan 3, 2 pts. Oxford: Clarendon Press, 1962.

Barthélemy, D., and J. T. Milik. *Qumran Cave I*. Discoveries in the Judaean Desert 1. Oxford: Clarendon Press, 1955.

Baumgarten, J. M. "4Q Halaka[a] 5, the Law of Ḥadash, and the Pentacontad Calendar." *JSS* 27 (1976) 36–46.

———. "On the Testimony of Women in 1QSa." *JBL* 76 (1957) 266–69. Reprinted in his *Studies in Qumran Law*. Leiden: E. J. Brill, 1977.

———. "Qumran Studies." *JBL* 77 (1958) 249–57.

———. "Sacrifice and Worship among the Jewish Sectarians of the Dead Sea (Qumran) Scrolls." *HTR* 46 (1953) 141–57.

Beasley-Murray, G. R. *Jesus and the Kingdom of God*. Grand Rapids: Eerdmans, 1986.

Ben-Sira. See Segal, M. H.

Bokser, B. "Approaching Sacred Space." *HTR* 78 (1985) 279–99.

———. "A Minor for *Zimmun* (Y. Ber. 7:2, 11c) and Recensions of Yerushalmi." *AJSR* 4 (1979) 1–25.

———. *Origins of the Seder*. Berkeley, Los Angeles and London: University of California Press, 1984.

———. "Philo's Description of Jewish Practices." *Protocol of the Thirtieth Colloquy: 5 June 1977*. Berkeley: Center for Hermeneutical Studies, 1977.

Bowman, J. "Did the Qumran Sect Burn the Red Heifer?" *RQ* 1 (1958) 73–84.

Brown, F., S. Driver, and C. Briggs. *A Hebrew and English Lexicon of the Old Testament.* Oxford: Oxford University Press, 1966.

Brown, R. E. "The Messianism of Qumran." *CBQ* 19 (1957) 53–82.

Burrows, M., J. C. Trevor, and W. H. Brownlee. *The Dead Sea Scrolls of Saint Mark's Monastery,* vol. 2, Fascicle 2. New Haven: American Schools of Oriental Research, 1951.

Caragounis, C. *The Son of Man: Vision and Interpretation.* Tübingen: J. C. B. Mohr, 1986.

Carmignac, J. "Quelques détails de lecture." *RQ* 4 (1963–64) 83–96.

———. *La Règle de la guerre.* Paris: Letouzey et Ané, 1958.

———, É. Cothenet, and H. Lignée. *Les Textes de Qumran.* 2 vols. Paris: Letouzey et Ané, 1961, 1963.

Caro, J. שולחן ערוך. 10 vols. New York: M. P. Press, 1967.

Charles, R. H. *The Apocrypha and Pseudepigrapha of the Old Testament.* 2 vols. Oxford: Clarendon Press, 1913.

———. *The Ethiopic Version of the Hebrew Book of Jubilees.* Oxford: Clarendon Press, 1895.

Collins, J. J. *The Apocalyptic Imagination.* New York: Crossroad, 1984.

———. "Messianism in the Maccabean Period." *Judaisms and their Messiahs.* Edited by J. Neusner, W. S. Green and E. Frerichs. Cambridge: Cambridge University Press, 1988.

Cross, F. M. *The Ancient Library at Qumran.* Garden City, New York: Doubleday, 1961.

Delcor, M. "Repas cultuels Esséniens et Thérapeutes, Thiases et Ḥaburoth." *RQ* 6 (1967–69) 401–25.

Drazin, N. *A History of Jewish Education.* Baltimore: Johns Hopkins Press, 1940.

Duhaime, J.-L. "Remarques sur les dépôts d'ossements d'animaux à Qumrân." *RQ* 9 (1977–78) 245–51.

Enṣiqlopedyah Talmudit. 17 vols. (to date). Jerusalem: Talmudic Encyclopedia, 1973–.

Epstein, J. N. מבוא לנוסח המשנה. 2 vols. Jerusalem, Tel Aviv: Magnes Press, 1963–64.

———. "שרידי שאילתות." *Tarbiz* 8 (1936–37) 5–54.

Fitzmyer, J. A. *Essays on the Semitic Background of the New Testament.* London: Geoffrey Chapman, 1974.

Gärtner, B. *The Temple and the Community in Qumran and the New Testament.* Cambridge: Cambridge University Press, 1965.

Ginsberg, H. L. "Messiah." *EJ* 11. 1407–8.

Ginzberg, L. *The Legends of the Jews*. Philadelphia: Jewish Publication Society, 1968.

———. *An Unknown Jewish Sect*. New York: Jewish Theological Seminary, 1971.

Goldstein, J. A. "How the Authors of 1 and 2 Maccabees Treated the 'Messianic' Promises." *Judaisms and Their Messiahs at the Turn of the Christian Era*. Edited by J. Neusner, W. S. Green and E. S. Frerichs. Cambridge: Cambridge University Press, 1987.

Gombiner, Abraham Abele ben Hayyim Ha-Levi. "מגן אברהם" in J. Caro, שולחן ערוך. 10 vols. New York: M. P. Press, 1967.

Gordis, R. "The 'Begotten' Messiah in the Qumran Scrolls." *VT* 7 (1957) 191–94.

Green, W. S. "Introduction: Messiah in Judaism: Rethinking the Question." *Judaisms and Their Messiahs at the Turn of the Christian Era*. Edited by J. Neusner, W. S. Green and E. S. Frerichs. Cambridge: Cambridge University Press, 1987.

Guilbert, P. "Le plan de la 'Règle de la Communauté.'" *RQ* 1 (1958–59) 323–44.

Halivni, D. מקורות ומסורות, סדר מועד. Jerusalem: Jewish Theological Seminary, 1974–75.

Jongeling, B. *Le Rouleau de la guerre*. Assen: Van Gorcum, 1962.

Josephus. [*Works*]. Translated by H. St. J. Thackeray, R. Marcus, A. Wikgren, and L. Feldman. 9 vols. Cambridge, MA: Harvard University Press, London: William Heinemann, 1926–65.

Kasher, M. תורה שלמה, vol. 27. Jerusalem: American Biblical Encyclopedia Society, 1975.

Kautzsch, E. *Gesenius' Hebrew Grammar*. Translated by A. E. Cowley. Oxford: Clarendon Press, 1910.

Klinzing, G. *Die Umdeutung des Kultus in der Qumrangemeinde und im Neuen Testament*. Göttingen: Vandenhoeck & Ruprecht, 1971.

Kraus, S. פרס ורומי. Jerusalem: Mosad Harav Kook, 1948.

Kuhn, K. G. "The Lord's Supper and the Communal Meal at Qumran." *The Scrolls and the New Testament*. Edited by K. Stendahl, London: SCM Press, 1958.

———. "The Two Messiahs of Aaron and Israel." *The Scrolls and the New Testament*. Edited by K. Stendahl, London: SCM Press, 1958.

Kutscher, E. Y. הלשון והרקע הלשוני של מגילת ישעיהו השלמה ממגילות ים המלח. Jerusalem: Magnes Press, 1959.

Laperrousaz, E. M. "A propos des dépôts d'ossements d'animaux trouvés à Qoumrân." *RQ* 9 (1977–78) 569–73.

————. *Qoumrân, l'établissement Essénien des bords de la Mer Morte.* Paris: A. & J. Picard, 1976.

Levine, B. A. "The Temple Scroll: Aspects of its Historical Provenance and Literary Character." *BASOR* 232 (1978) 5–23.

Licht, J. "An Analysis of the Treatise of the Two Spirits in DSD." *Aspects of the Dead Sea Scrolls.* Scripta Hierosolymitana 4. Edited by C. Rabin and Y. Yadin. Jerusalem: Magnes Press, 1958.

————. "Day of the Lord." *EJ* 5. 1387–88.

————. "אל פדות ועם עולם מטעת" in הגנוזות במגילות מחקרים. Edited by Y. Yadin and C. Rabin. Jerusalem: Hekhal Ha-Sefer, 1961.

————. ההודיות מגילת. Jerusalem: Bialik Institute, 1957.

————. הסרכים מגילת. Jerusalem: Mosad Bialik, 1965.

Liddell, H., and R. Scott. *A Greek-English Lexicon.* Revised and augmented by H. Stuart Jones and R. McKenzie, with a Supplement. Oxford: Oxford University Press, 1968.

Lieberman, S. כפשוטה תוספתא. 8 vols. New York: Jewish Theological Seminary, 1955–.

————. "The Discipline in the So-Called Dead Sea Manual of Discipline." *JBL* 71 (1952) 199–206.

Lightstone, J. N. *Yose the Galilean,* vol. 1. Leiden: E. J. Brill, 1979.

Lipschutz, I. ישראל תפארת in *Mishnah.* Vilna edition. 12 vols. New York: Pardes, 1952–53.

Liver, J. "יהודה מדבר במגילות השקל מחצית." *Tarbiz* 31 (1960–61) 18–22.

————. "השקל מחצית פרשת." *Y. Kaufmann Jubilee Volume.* Edited by M. Haran. Jerusalem: Magnes Press, 1960–61.

Lohse, E. *Die Texte aus Qumran.* Munich: Kösel-Verlag, 1986.

Maimonides, M. תורה משנה. Warsaw-Vilna edition. 5 vols. Jerusalem: Pardes, 1955.

————. המשניות פרוש. In *Mishnah,* Codex Parma "C." Naples: 1492, and *Babylonian Talmud.* 20 vols. New York: Otzar Hasefarim, 1964.

————. המשניות פירוש. In מימון בן משה רבנו פירוש עם משנה. Edited and translated by J. Kafah. 3 vols. Jerusalem: Mossad Harav Kook, 1963.

————. המצות ספר. Edited by H. Heller. Jerusalem: Mossad Harav Kook, 1979–80.

Maier, J. *Die Texte vom Toten Meer.* 2 vols. Munich and Basel: Ernst Reinhardt, 1960.

————. *The Temple Scroll.* Journal for the Study of the Old Testament — Supplement Series 34. Sheffield: University of Sheffield, 1985.

Martin, M. *The Scribal Character of the Dead Sea Scrolls.* 2 vols. Louvain: Institut Orientaliste, 1958.

Mekhilta' De-Rabbi Ishmael. Edited by H. S. Horovitz and I. A. Rabin. Jerusalem: Bamberger and Wahrmann, 1960.

Mekhilta' De-Rabbi Shim'on ben Yoḥai. Edited by J. N. Epstein and E. Z. Melamed. Jerusalem: Mekize Nirdamim, 1955.

Mekhilta' De-Rabbi Shim'on ben Yoḥai. Edited by D. Hoffmann. Frankfurt a. M.: J. Kaufmann, 1905.

Midrash Ha-Gadol. Edited by S. Fisch. Jerusalem: Mossad Harav Kook, 1972.

Midrash Rabbah. Vilna edition. 2 vols. New York: Grossman, 1952.

Milgrom, J. "Studies in the Temple Scroll." *JBL* 97 (1978) 512–18.

———. "'Sabbath' and 'Temple City' in the Temple Scroll." *BASOR* 232 (1978) 25–27.

Milik, J. T. "The Manual of Discipline by P. Wernberg-Møller." (review) *RB* 67 (1960) 410–16.

———. *Ten Years of Discovery in the Wilderness of Judaea.* London: SCM Press, 1959.

Mishnah. Vilna edition. 12 vols. New York: Pardes, 1952–53.

Moore, G. F. *Judaism.* 2 vols. New York: Schocken, 1971.

Mowinckel, S. *He that Cometh.* Translated by G. W. Anderson. Oxford: Basil Blackwell, 1956.

Nebe, G. W. "Der Gebrauch der sogennanten nota accusativi את in Damaskusschrift XV, 5.9 und 12." *RQ* 8 (1973) 257–64.

Neusner, J. *Early Rabbinic Judaism.* Leiden: E. J. Brill, 1975.

———. "Emergent Rabbinic Judaism in a Time of Crisis." *Judaism* 21 (1979) 313–27.

———. *A History of the Mishnaic Law of Holy Things.* Part III. Leiden: E. J. Brill, 1979.

Newton, M. *The Concept of Purity at Qumran and in the Letters of Paul.* Society for New Testament Studies Monograph Series 53. Cambridge: Cambridge University Press, 1985.

Nickelsburg, G. W. E. "Salvation without and with a Messiah: Developing Beliefs in Writings Ascribed to Enoch." *Judaisms and Their Messiahs at the Turn of the Christian Era.* Edited by J. Neusner, W. S. Green and E. S. Frerichs. Cambridge: Cambridge University Press, 1987.

Nissim ben Reuven Gerondi. Commentary to *b. Nedarim.* In *Babylonian Talmud.* Vilna edition. 20 vols. New York: Otzar Hasefarim, 1964.

Nolland, J. "A Misleading Statement of the Essene Attitude to the Temple." *RQ* 9 (1977–78) 555–62.

North, R. "Qumran 'Serek a' and Related Fragments." *Orientalia* 25 (1956) 90–99.

Numbers Rabbah in *Midrash Rabbah*. Vilna edition. 2 vols. New York: Grossman, 1961–62.

Oppenheimer, A. *The 'Am Ha-'Aretz*. Leiden: E. J. Brill, 1977.

Palestinian Talmud. Krotoschin edition. Jerusalem: Torah La-'Am, 1959–60.

Palestinian Talmud. Zhitomir edition (with commentaries). 5 vols. Jerusalem: Bene Ma'arav, 1979–80.

Peck, A. J. *The Priestly Gift in Mishnah*. Chico, CA: Scholars Press, 1981.

Philo. [*Works*]. Edited and translated by F. H. Colson, G. H. Whitaker, and R. Marcus. 10 vols. and 2 supplementary vols. Cambridge, MA: Harvard University Press, 1929–53.

Ploeg, J. van der, "The Meals of the Essenes." *JSS* 2 (1957) 163–75.

Porton, G. *The Traditions of Rabbi Ishmael*. 3 vols. Leiden: E. J. Brill, 1976–79.

Preuss, J. *Biblical and Talmudic Medicine*. Translated by F. Rosner. New York, London: Sanhedrin Press, 1978.

Priest, J. F. "The Messiah and the Meal in 1QSa." *JBL* 82 (1963) 95–100.

Pseudo-Rashi. See Solomon ben Isaac (Pseudo-).

Qimron, E. *The Hebrew of the Dead Sea Scrolls*. Harvard Semitic Studies 29. Atlanta, GA: Scholars Press, 1986.

Rabin, C. *The Zadokite Documents*. Oxford: Oxford University Press, 1954.

Ran. See Nissim ben Reuven Gerondi.

Rashi. See Solomon ben Isaac.

Richardson, H. N. "Some Notes on 1QSa." *JBL* 76 (1957) 108–22.

Ringgren, H. *The Faith of Qumran*. Philadelphia: Fortress Press, 1963.

Sarason, R. *A History of the Mishnaic Law of Agriculture*. Part 3, vol. 1. Leiden: E.J. Brill, 1979.

Schechter, S. *Documents of Jewish Sectaries*. 2 vols. in 1, with "Prolegomenon" by J. A. Fitzmyer. New York: Ktav, 1970.

Schiffman, L. H. "The Concept of the Messiah in Second Temple and Rabbinic Literature." *Review and Expositor* 84 (1987) 235–46.

———. "The Dead Sea Scrolls and the Early History of Jewish Liturgy." In *The Synagogue in Late Antiquity*. Edited by L. I. Levine. Philadelphia: American Schools of Oriental Research, 1987.

———. "Exclusion from the Sanctuary and the City of the Sanctuary in the Temple Scroll." *Biblical and Other Studies in Memory of S. D. Goitein*. Hebrew Annual Review 9. Edited by R. Ahroni. Columbus: Ohio State University, 1985.

———. *The Halakhah at Qumran*. Leiden: E. J. Brill, 1975.

———. "The Impurity of the Dead in the Temple Scroll." To appear in *Archaeology and History in the Dead Sea Scrolls. The New York University*

Conference in Memory of Yigael Yadin. Edited by L. H. Schiffman. American Schools of Oriental Research.

———. "Jewish Sectarianism in Second Temple Times." *Great Schisms in Jewish History*. Edited by R. Jospe and S. M. Wagner. New York: Ktav, 1981.

———. "The Laws of War in the Temple Scroll." In *Mémorial Jean Carmignac*. Edited by F. García Martínez and É. Puech. *RQ* 13 (1988) 300–302.

———. "Legislation concerning Relations with non-Jews in the *Zadokite Fragments* and in Tannaitic Literature." *RQ* 11 (1983) 379–89.

———. "*Merkavah* Speculation at Qumran: The 4Q *Serekh Shirot* 'Olat ha-Shabbat." In *Mystics, Philosophers, and Politicians, Essays in Honor of Alexander Altmann*. Edited by J. Reinharz and D. Swetschinski with K. P. Bland. Durham, NC: Duke University Press, 1982.

———. "Messianic Figures and Ideas in the Qumran Scrolls." To appear in *The Messiah*. Anchor Bible Reference Library. Garden City: Doubleday. Edited by J. H. Charlesworth.

———. "The Sacrificial System of The *Temple Scroll* and the Book of Jubilees." In *Society of Biblical Literature 1985 Seminar Papers*. Edited by K. H. Richards. Society of Biblical Literature Seminar Papers Series 24. Atlanta, GA: Scholars Press, 1985.

———. *Sectarian Law in the Dead Sea Scrolls, Courts, Testimony, and the Penal Code*. Brown Judaic Studies 33. Chico, CA: Scholars Press, 1983.

Scholem, G. "Toward an Understanding of the Messianic Idea in Judaism." *The Messianic Idea in Judaism*. New York: Schocken Books, 1971.

Schürer, E. *The History of the Jewish People in the Age of Jesus Christ*. 3 vols. in 4. Edited by G. Vermes and F. Millar. Edinburgh: T. & T. Clark, 1973–1987.

Schwartz, D. "סופרים ופרושים חנפים—מי הם 'הסופרים' בברית החדשה?" *Zion* 50 (1984–85) 121–32.

Segal, M. H. ספר בן סירא השלם. Jerusalem: Mosad Bialik, 1971–72.

———. "ספר ברית דמשק." *Ha-Shiloah* 26 (1912) 390–406, 483–506.

Sifra' De-Ve Rav (Torat Kohanim). Edited by I. H. Weiss. Vienna: J. Schlossberg, 1861–62.

Sifre De-Ve Rav (Numbers). Edited by H. S. Horovitz. Jerusalem: Wahrmann, 1966.

Sifre on Deuteronomy. Edited by L. Finkelstein. New York: Jewish Theological Seminary, 1969.

Sifre Zuṭa'. In *Sifre De-Ve Rav (Numbers)*. Edited by H. S. Horovitz. Jerusalem: Wahrmann, 1966.

Skehan, P. "Two Books on Qumran Studies." *CBQ* 21 (1959) 71–78.

Smith, M. "God's Begetting the Messiah in 1 Q Sa." *NTS* 5 (1958–59) 218–24.

Smith, W. R. *The Religion of the Semites.* New York: Schocken, 1972.

Solomon ben Isaac (and Pseudo-). Commentary to the *Babylonian Talmud.* In *Babylonian Talmud.* Vilna edition. 20 vols. New York: Otzar Hasefarim, 1964.

Sutcliffe, E. F. "The Rule of the Congregation (1QSa) II, 11–12: Text and Meaning." *RQ* 2 (1959–60) 541–47.

Talmon, S. "The 'Desert Motif' in the Bible and Qumran Literature." *Biblical Motifs.* Edited by A. Altmann, Cambridge: Harvard University Press, 1966.

———. *King, Cult, and Calendar in Ancient Israel.* Jerusalem: Magnes Press, the Hebrew University, 1986.

———. "Waiting for the Messiah: The Spiritual Universe of the Qumran Covenanters." *Judaisms and Their Messiahs at the Turn of the Christian Era.* Edited by J. Neusner, W. S. Green and E. S. Frerichs. Cambridge: Cambridge University Press, 1987.

Targum Pseudo-Jonathan. Edited by H. Ginsburger. Berlin: S. Calvary, 1903.

The Torah. Philadelphia: Jewish Publication Society of America, 1962.

Vaux, R. de. *Archaeology and the Dead Sea Scrolls.* London: Oxford University Press, 1973.

Wernberg-Møller, P. *The Manual of Discipline.* Leiden: E. J. Brill, 1957.

Yadin, Y. "A Crucial Passage in the Dead Sea Scrolls." *JBL* 78 (1959) 238–41.

———. "Is the Temple Scroll a Sectarian Document?" *Humanizing America's Iconic Book: Society of Biblical Literature Centennial Addresses, 1980.* Edited by G. M. Tucker and D. A. Knight. Chico, CA: Scholars Press, 1982.

———. *The Scroll of the War of the Sons of Light against the Sons of Darkness.* Oxford: Oxford University Press, 1962.

———. *The Temple Scroll.* 3 vols. and 1 vol. of supplementary plates. Jerusalem: Israel Exploration Society, 1983.

Yalon, H. מגילות מדבר יהודה. Jerusalem: Shrine of the Book Fund and Kiryath Sepher, 1967.

INDEX OF TEXTS CITED

HEBREW SCRIPTURES

QUMRAN LITERATURE

APOCRYPHA

PSEUDEPIGRAPHA

PHILO AND JOSEPHUS

NEW TESTAMENT

RABBINIC LITERATURE

Mishnah

Tosefta

Palestinian Talmud

INDEX OF HEBREW AND ARAMAIC TERMS

INDEX OF MODERN
AUTHORS CITED

INDEX OF SUBJECTS

Reviews

B. Z. Wacholder, JBL 110/1 (1991) 147-48.
G. J. Brooke, JSS 38/1 (1993) 149-50.